MW01255205

"Get ready for a r
a girl growing up
Matters: True Tale.
Life, Karen Brother
adolescence, from th   ...including ner mother's fight
against cancer. Brothers has a wonderful eye for detail and captures the
glorious era of malls, perms, and shoulder pads. Moreover, by reflecting
on the spark of life that continues after great sadness, Brothers highlights
the resilience and magic within us all. Karen Brothers' Moxie Matters is a
must-read for anyone who loves a good coming-of-age story filled with the
"messy, muddled, and magical" aspects of life."

Dr. Martha Amore
Assistant Professor, Department of Writing, University of Alaska, Anchorage,
Karen's High School Friend

"There is so much charm, humor, and sweet nostalgia in this memoir that
you almost don't grasp the depth of emotions behind each chapter until
they sneak up on you and stop you in your tracks. Even if you don't know
this girl sharing her story…you know this girl. You can see her. Hear her.
Understand her. Cringe for her. Laugh with her. Feel with her. Cheer for
her. In the end, you might even feel you ARE her to some degree, her story
and the remarkably beautiful way she tells it is that universally relatable.
I cannot recommend this read highly enough!"

Erin Noel Grennan
Stage and Television Actor/Writer,
Fellow alto in Karen's high school choir and friend

"Karen is an amazing storyteller. Her life experience wrapped in story is
a great read."

Steffani LeFevour
Happiness Coach, Author of *You are a Badass Mom*,
Karen's high school friend

"This memoir is a testament to the power of sharing stories. Captivatingly
honest, Moxie Matters will take you to a place where immense joy and
unbearable grief coincide. You will revel in Karen's accomplishments,
finding inspiration in every milestone she achieves and every barrier she
breaks down."

Grace Harvey
Middle School Social Studies Teacher, Volleyball Coach, Book Lover,
Karen's niece and Goddaughter

"I first met Karen while dog sitting for their sweet angel Molly. I went over
to learn her care routine and what could have been a 30 minute walk
through turned into an hour and a half discussion on life. I left knowing
two things: Wow, Karen is really cool and she is an amazing storyteller.
Moxie Matters perfectly encapsulates Karen's amazing ability to connect
with others through empathy, openness, and storytelling."

Catie Snowden
Lover of Books, Content Creator @caties.curated.collection on Instagram,
Karen's preferred dog sitter and friend

"Moxie Matters is pure delight. The energy and joy that little Karen exudes is palpable. And that same sweet, enthusiastic energy follows her as she grows up. Karen Brothers' magical memory of hilarious, fun and meaningful details remind me of best-selling author, Kelly Corrigan's The Middle Place. You will smile and be inspired as you read this page-turner of a memoir."

Jessica Patay
Host of "Brave Together" podcast, Executive Director of We Are Brave Together

"Karen has captured her childhood in a time capsule collection of vivid memories of growing up in the 70's and 80's. Her vignettes are at once delightful, hilarious, deeply poignant and genuine. Her humor masterfully draws you into each childhood recollection as if you were there and reveals how it feels to navigate through life's ups and downs. Beautifully written and a must read!"

Julie Utter
Mission-Driven, Lover-of-Books, Karen's friend

"Moxie Matters is so fun. I love the hutzpah in Karen, throughout her young life, and continuing into adulthood."

Staci Kaufmannn Muller
Jeweler, Karen's friend and partner in crime

"Karen Brothers has a unique gift for sharing the magical and the messy with sparkle. This book is an open invitation to reflect on our own stories as we connect with others around us."

Dawn Weisto
Avid book reader, Advocate, Karen's friend and shenanigan sidekick

"I'm not sure if my drying tears are from laughing or crying. Either way, I feel Karen, and I remember what it's like growing up. It seems she feels me too. Karen is a great story storyteller, and though I met her after all these shenanigans, I'm lucky to know and love this Karen and how she connects to others through shared life experiences. Wish I had her moxie!"

Linda McGee
Writer, Artist, Consultant, Karen's friend

"Moxie Matters is a heartwarming journey through the highs and lows of growing up, capturing the essence of childhood adventures, teenage trials, and the poignant moments that shape us. With humor, grace, and a touch of nostalgia, Karen invites readers onto a rollercoaster of life in the Chicago suburbs, reminding us of the enduring strength of spirit and the magic of memories. A truly captivating read that echoes the laughter, tears, and moxie of our own lives."

Dana L. Halle
Esq., Songwriter, Nonprofit leader, Karen's light writing friend

KAREN BROTHERS

MOXIE MATTERS

True Tales of Rolling Through
a Messy, Muddled, and
Magical Life

First Print Edition, 2024
Printed in China

Publishing Services: Jodi Cowles, Brandon Janous, and Rachael Mitchell (Blue Hat Publishing)
Cover Design & Interior Layout: Tim Marshall (Blue Hat Publishing)
All photos courtesy of Karen Brothers
ISBN (print): 978-1-962674-04-1
ISBN (ebook): 978-1-962674-05-8

Names, identifying details, and locations have been altered to protect the privacy of individuals and entities. Real-life events and locales are portrayed within the confines of the author's memory and recollection, subject to the inherent limitations of personal perspective and interpretation.

The author acknowledges that memory can be fallible and that the portrayal of events, conversations, and circumstances within this memoir may differ from others' recollections or historical records. No harm or defamation is intended toward any person, group, or entity mentioned in this work.

BLUE HAT
PUBLISHING
BOISE · KNOXVILLE · NASHVILLE · SEATTLE
WWW.BLUEHATPUBLISHING.COM

To my daughters **Courtney, Kaylyn**, and **Olivia,**
you are the best stories I have ever created.
I love you so much and am proud we are THAT family.

To **Mike Brothers**, I love you. You are my favorite.

KAREN BROTHERS

Preface

All of humanity is connected. I believe we are connected through the work of the Holy Spirit. But for you, it might be something else. I respect whatever you believe. Because we are all connected, it is important to share our stories. When we do, people relate to our stories, thus further extending the threads of connection. Maybe my story will help you to see that you are not alone in yours. Our stories won't be identical, but maybe, just maybe, one piece of my story will touch you, and pull us together. And then you might share your story with someone else and make a connection.

Stories matter. For years I have felt compelled to share my stories; this book has been in the works for a while. My stories have been pushing to be told. At times I wrote each story as an essay, unsure of what to do with them. I took a break from my essays and started a fiction novel, soon realizing the main character of my novel was me. Thank you for choosing to read them and I deeply hope a piece of me connects with a piece of you, thus connecting us and empowering you to tell your stories, too.

MO·XIE: [mok-see] *noun*

1. Force of character, determination, or nerve. "When you've got moxie, you need the clothes to match."

Synonyms: energy, pep, determination, courage, know-how, fortitude, savvy, skills, strength of mind, guts, fearlessness, heart, gumption.

MARCH 17, 1970

The day I am born, my parents drop my three-year-old brother and five-year-old sister off at the neighbor's house two doors down. Patricia and Carl O'Rourke have an annual St. Patrick's Day party, and the revelers are happy to have two young kids without parents added into the mix.

My sister wanders the party and enjoys the activity. My brother is terrified and chooses to sit in a kitchen cupboard for the duration of the festivities.

After I am born, a variety of neighborhood women—all named Patricia—asked my mom how on earth she failed to name me "After the blessed St. Patrick" because "I was blessed to be born on his feast day." She replies that she is a German Lutheran and Karen Melissa is my name.

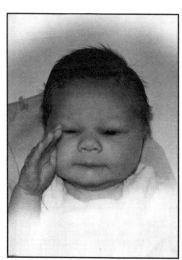

Lenox Street, Oak Park, Illinois

My parents bring me home to a modest two-story brick bungalow which is what most midwestern, middle-class families strive for in the Chicago suburbs. It's not open-concept like the fabulous Brady house and there are no sweeping stairwells but it's comfortable and our now family of five fits well. There are four bedrooms, two full baths, and an unfinished basement that runs the length of the house.

The "front" room, also sometimes called the living room, is the largest space on the first floor. It has leaded glass windows and lots of light. An electric fireplace flanks one wall and a gorgeous, six foot long, wooden stereo cabinet flanks the other. This is no ordinary stereo cabinet. It can not only store albums and 8-track cassettes, but it plays both as well. The two speakers on either end are covered in high-tech cloth that allows the sound to fill the room while the decorated wooden carvings over it show just the right touch of class. Light green shag carpet flows, lending an element of 70's sophistication.

The formal dining room feels like the heartbeat of the home. It is fancy and all-important family, friend, and neighborhood functions happen here. In the wintertime, the radiator is the perfect spot to dry damp scarves, mittens, and hats, or curl up with a homemade afghan to warm frozen bones after playing out in the snow for hours.

Beyond the dining room is the kitchen. There is a little desk area where the built-in, round dining table flattens out for a little workspace. It is all connected to the wall with a pedestal base underneath and room for five swivel chairs. Our gold telephone hangs on the wall right there and this is my mom's workspace. The wall opposite the entryway houses the back door which leads to a small screened-in porch and our all-cement backyard. This is home.

First Memory, 1971

There is very little light. I'm sitting up in my crib. Across the room, the door opens slowly and a slice of light folds in. It opens just a bit more and then it is quickly closed. I blink and know who is here. My big brother, David, not five years old, has come into my room. I'm happy as he walks over to my crib, and we touch hands. He starts to fiddle with first one bar, and then another, as he somehow pulls them right out. When there is enough room, I lean forward, and he pulls me out of my crib. I feel safe and really, really, happy. I love my brother!

Pet Store, 1974

I stand at the closed door to David's bedroom, one of Mommy's old purses on my shoulder, full of all the pretend money from the Monopoly game. I feel wobbly on my play high heels, and I can't stop giggling. I love to pretend!

I open the door and in a very grown-up voice, I say, "Hello dah-lings! I am here at your pet store to buy a new pet!"

As I walk around the store, I see little kitties, and doggies. They are all so cute. How can I pick?

"Ruff ruff!"

There is a very happy puppy here wagging his tail and barking for me. He is so cute! I pat his head.

"Hello cute little puppy! I think I will buy you and take you home to live with me forever."

I grab the belt/leash near the cash register and loop it around this happy puppy's neck. Now I need to pay.

"Come on little puppy, let's pay for you!"

I hand over all the money in my purse to the pretend cashier and walk my happy puppy out the door, and across the hall to my home. I take off the belt/leash and we play fetch and I feed him a snack and water from bowls on my floor. I love my puppy!

David and I play this game over and over. He pretends to be different kinds of animals, but he is always happy, and it is fun to buy him and take him home to play!

The Summer of 1975

I stand under the basketball net in the backyard and watch as my groom pedals his chunky little legs off as he arrives at our wedding in style on his new Green Machine. The Green Machine is a step up from the basic Big Wheel. Thomas sits in the big black seat, and there are gears to use as he pedals and steers toward his future…as my soon-to-be husband.

My big sister, Sue, decided it was time for a wedding in the neighborhood and she arranges everything. We have a bride costume in the Halloween bin and she helps me fluff the tattered, yet beautiful, veil on my head. I pull some dandelions from the mud under the basketball net and wait with Sue holding a Bible, as my favorite person and best friend makes a sharp right turn up the driveway from his house, five doors down.

Right as Thomas gets to the sewer in the backyard, he dramatically slams on his brakes, using the hand levers. Before stepping off of this wondrous vehicle he has just gotten as a birthday gift, he pulls up both of his tube socks, all the way to his knees. They are a little bit big and the heel part sticks out at the back. As the youngest of four boys, he is doing his best with hand-me-downs.

He looks at Sue and rolls his eyes.

"Okay Thomas, you're the groom! It's time for the wedding!"

He walks up to me, nods his head, and the ceremony begins. Just minutes later, it is complete! By the power vested in my sister, by my sister, and with a few other neighbor kids present as witnesses, I am married to my first ever husband!

Within moments we hear his mom from their back porch.

"Tho-mas! Lunch is ready!"

And quick as a wink, my new husband jumps on his awesome Green Machine and peels right back down the driveway, hanging that sharp left at the sidewalk.

"Bye, Karen!"

"Bye, Husband!"

It is days before the start of kindergarten, and I am so happy What a great way to start school—with a new husband!

Kindergarten
1975-1976

Miss Jones looks like a bird. Her pointy chin blocks my view to her equally pointy nose, forming a perfect beak. The skinny legs that stick out from her corduroy jumper are stick-like and I swear she could take flight at any moment and swoop down onto any of the students she pecks at throughout the day.

Walking into the classroom is wonderful. As I enter, I can't even see clearly to the other end of the room. Directly to the right is a large, carpeted area with a solid wooden rocking chair. Straight ahead is an actual metal jungle gym—inside the classroom. Magnificent! On my left side is a door that leads to a bathroom with a tiny, just-my-size toilet. It is almost too much to take in. Closing my eyes, the smell of rubber cement mixes with the heady scent of paints at the ready, placed in front of individual easels with blank paper clipped to the top of each. What will I paint first? My Barbies? My stuffed animal friends? Maybe my family? So many things to paint!

Past the art center and jungle gym are tiny tables and chairs. Hooks are on the walls with the names of each student above their very own. Over the hooks are smooth, wooden cubbies to hold book bags, hats, scarves, and treasured future show-and-tell items. This is a magical room, and I am ready for all that it has to offer.

All three Modder kids are in the same building for this whole year. My older brother, David, is on the second floor with the other fourth graders. Sue, the oldest, is all the way up on the third floor in her sixth-grade class. The third floor! I can't even dream of what is happening up there with all the biggest kids in the school. I am on the first floor and glad to have a little space to figure out this thing called school.

Miss Jones loves her perch in the rocking chair at what is called Circle Time. Each day, she will call all the children over and we can choose our own seat—as long as our bottom is touching an edge of the carpet. I always sit next to my best friend, neighbor, and new husband, Thomas O'Neill. We are inseparable.

One day, Miss Jones is reading the class a story at Circle Time. As her squawking goes on, I get bored. With a smile on my face, I start poking Thomas. He looks at me and scrunches up his face, and I think he wants me to stop. Making Thomas laugh is one of my favorite things to do and I can't help myself. I have to get him to laugh. I full-on start to tickle him until he falls over on his side, the giggles spilling right out of him.

Miss Jones stops reading and the room gets very quiet, very fast. She rises from her chair and stands right in front of us. Her black eyes stare right through me, and I swallow my laughter right down. My punishment is to sit directly under her chair as she continues with the story. Yes, that's right. The only adult in the room puts little troublemaking me directly under her chair where she cannot see me, but my classmates can.

Now, Oak Park District 97 is well known and should attract only the best and brightest. I'm not quite sure how Miss Jones slipped in.

Five-year-old me is now under her chair with a full audience in front of me. It feels so great to make Thomas laugh, and I wonder what I could possibly do now that every one of my classmates is looking straight at me. I stick my thumbs into the corners of my mouth and take my middle fingers right into my nostrils and pull with all of my might as I open my eyes as wide as they could go and cross them. This is a new funny face I have been practicing for days!

I then flap my arm like a bird and hobble back and forth on my bottom, mimicking Miss Jones as she reads. It works. My audience starts smiling, and then they laugh. They laugh out loud and I love it! It doesn't last long enough. Miss Jones stands and bends down facing me. She pulls me out from under her chair.

Grabbing my arm, she guides me to the hallway. Her nostrils are flaring as she attempts to catch her breath. Why is she breathing so hard? I am scared now. Mr. Donaldson, our beloved principal, might see me out here. The hallway is for actual naughty children. I am not naughty—I am funny! This is a big problem. I slide down onto my tiny kindergarten bottom with my back against the wall. I close my eyes and hold my breath, hoping to become invisible.

It doesn't work.

"Miss Modder? Is that you? Open your eyes, Miss Modder."

I peek one eye open and there he is. The wonderful, mustached, Mr. Donaldson who drives his bike past our house twice a day, to and from work. His smile is bright and white and makes a person feel happy. He always wears a tie and a rubber band around his pant leg so it won't get caught in his bike chain. I believe he actually truly loves children and I bet his hugs smell like my dad's soap on a rope.

"Miss Modder, why are you sitting in the hallway?"

Just as I am about to answer, I hear a loud gasp. My brother is also in the hallway! What is he doing on the first floor? I close my eyes again. Surely this will make me invisible. Nope. He sees me sitting there and our principal squatting down in front of me. Oh no, I am really going to get in trouble now. It is bad enough that Mr. Donaldson sees me, but Dave will tell Mom and Dad for sure. I am really going to be in trouble. Mr. Donaldson looks over at my brother and waits until he walks away to look back at my stricken face.

As the tears begin to spill down my cheeks, I respond, "I tickled Thomas during story time. Miss Jones didn't like it."

With a big exhale, my wonderful principal says, "Well, thank you for telling me the truth. I don't ever want to see you sitting out here again. Do you understand?"

"Yes, Mr. Donaldson, I understand."

Miss Jones definitely has it out for me because I can make the class laugh and she doesn't even know how to smile.

I love the sweet little bathroom with the just-my-size toilet in our classroom. I try to use it every single day, even if I don't really have to go. The acoustics are also spectacular, and I will occasionally sing a song, or two, while I try to go.

One day, as I am sitting on the tiny pot, elbows on my knees, hands curled under my chin contemplating my next song choice, my classmate Craig Andersen opens the door on me. I scream very, very loudly. This causes Craig to scream and slam the door. I think he runs clear past the jungle gym and is hiding somewhere in the art center.

Miss Jones quickly appears and raps solidly on the door.

"Just a minute!" I holler, "I'm not quite done yet."

"You ARE done. Now come on out right this minute."

I pull up my knit tights, pull down my red Snoopy jumper, take my time washing my hands, and finally open the door. I really hope Craig hasn't peed his pants from his hiding spot. Then the unthinkable happens. Miss Jones scolds ME for screaming. She tells me I am disruptive. I am shocked. What am I supposed to do? There are no tiny locks on the door. What is the proper response when Craig Andersen opens the door, and everyone around can see you sitting there with your naked butt on the toilet?

It doesn't matter. This time, she sends me straight to the principal's office.

I am angry as she holds my wrist and walks me the length of half a hallway to the office. I am scared and sad to be given what I consider to be such a severe punishment. Tears begin to fall as I wait in the grown-up-sized chair outside of Mr. Donaldson's office.

After I am led in, he asks me what happened.

"I was going tinkle on the potty and Craig Andersen opened the door and I screamed then he screamed then mean Miss Jones brought me here. I don't think she likes me."

"No, Miss Modder, I don't think she does."

Being sent to the principal is scary, but geez, I sure do like singing my brains out in the tiny kindergarten potty.

March 1976

I am so excited to go to Disney World! Miss Jones is not too happy that I am going to miss some of very important kindergarten to take a vacation. But she does not understand that this is an important trip with my aunt, uncle, and my cousins. Mom said she is ridiculous because she gave me more homework than my big brother and sister got and they are big kids. I don't even care because kindergarten homework is easy and I will do it all because I AM GOING TO DISNEY WORLD FOR MY BIRTHDAY!

I will turn six years old at Disney World. I am one lucky little girl.

Mom doesn't like to fly on airplanes, so I was picked to go with her on the Amtrak train. We have to leave a couple of days before Dad and Sue and Dave, but I don't care because it will be a good adventure.

It's the day of our trip and Mom has packed my suitcase for me. Dad takes us to the train and Mom holds my hand real tight while we are shown to our room. Mom says it is not a 'room,' but a place where we will sleep on our way to meet Mickey Mouse. I don't care what she wants to call it—I love it!

There is one, thin bed that takes up most of the room. I ask the guy showing us the place where the other bed for me is. He looks up, grabs a handle thing, and pulls down a cute little bed just for me! This is going to be amazing!

"Mom! Look at that! My own bed right up in the ceiling. I'm going to love it here!"

"Oh honey, we'll see. You might fall out. We can share this big bed."

"Mom, this is not a big bed. This is just enough room for one mom. I'm big enough for the cool bed. I promise."

"We'll see…"

Shoot. "We'll see" always means no way.

We get our suitcases all set. I love Mom's cool hard blue suitcase and matching train case. That little case holds all of her make-ups, perfumes, and all the things that make her so beautiful. I also like that it is small so I can carry it for her and show her what a big girl I am. Big enough to sleep in that drop-down bed.

"Let's go find the dining car."

Mom lights up a cigarette and we leave our little room to explore and find some lunch. The train rattles and shakes a little, but I can hardly tell we are moving. At the end of the car, we've got to open a door and walk through to the next car. Mom is scared and holds my hand too tight.

"Do not let go. Do you hear me? Do not let go of me and hurry across to the other side."

"Ouch, Mommy, okay, okay!"

We get through to the next car and have to do the scary-between-car move two more times before we get to the restaurant car. Mom is happy to be there and we order some lunch. She gets a Tab and I get a Coke. This is a fancy place! I put my cloth napkin on my lap and wait for my food to come. Mom is smoking and looking out the window. An old guy in a blue suit, with a nice hat, walks up and asks if he can sit with us. There aren't enough tables so I say yes before Mom gets a chance to.

She gives me the look. You know the look: eyes scrunched up making a wrinkly forehead and nose squishing up into the face. I don't think she is happy that I am sharing our table.

The old guy smiles and starts to chat.

"Thank you, young lady, for allowing me to sit with you and your mother. It does feel good to have a seat. The train sure is crowded."

Mom starts to nod.

"You're welcome mister! We are going to Disney World in Orlando, Florida. My mom is not going to get on an airplane, so we left early and are going to meet my dad, sister, brother, aunt, uncle, and my cousins in Orlando, Florida. We are going to be on a vacation! And on this vacation, I am going to have a birthday! I am going to be six years old on March 17, 1976. Isn't that neat?"

Mom rolls her eyes. Mister Old Guy laughs a little.

"Well that certainly sounds like a wonderful vacation! You are a lucky little girl."

"Don't I know it! We have never done a big vacation before in my life. I am so excited! And we have a sleeping room here on the train! There is a bed for my mom and a pull-down-from-the-ceiling bed for me. But Mom seems a little scared of that pull-down bed. I think she thinks it's going to swallow me up and shoot me out of the roof of the train or something. Isn't that funny? Then she'd wake up and be all alone and I'd be shot out somewhere from here to Orlando, Florida!"

Mom and I make friends with Mister Old Guy, and she says that he really is a delight. It turns out, he travels all over the world. He has friends in a lot of special places, and it makes him happy to go and visit them. We eat every meal with Mister Old Guy and every day he is wearing a nice suit with a cool hat. He always takes the hat off at eating time. He likes to listen to my stories, and I think Mom likes that she doesn't have to listen too much.

At the end of our train trip time, we share addresses with him and promise to be pen pals. I am excited to have a new friend. I love getting mail so much and I think I will be a good letter writer too. When it's time to leave, he shakes our hands and wishes me a very happy birthday.

What a trip! I am one lucky girl, and we haven't even gotten to Disney World yet!

Mom and I take a taxicab to the Polynesian Resort where we have our hotel room. And our room is going to have an actual door in the middle of the wall to connect to the cousin's room! My cousin Brenda is my best, best friend. She is in first grade and is exactly fifty weeks older than I am. I don't think she's too happy that we will be in Disney World for my birthday, and not hers. But the best part is that we get to be in Disney World, on a vacation, together!

We get to the hotel and wow, is it fancy. Mom says it's like a tropical paradise as she lights up a cigarette and takes my hand. We follow a worker guy who has our suitcases, and he takes us to our room. Mom and I got here first because the airplane with everyone else is coming later.

Mom decides she needs a little nap so while she climbs into bed, I go outside and sit on the balcony of our beautiful room. The room has two big beds and one couch that will pull out into a bed. Mom said that David will get his own bed and Sue and I will share. I sure hope we don't get the couch bed. Everyone knows couch beds are lumpy and hurt your body. Sometimes I sleep over at my cousin's, and we sleep on the couch bed in the TV room so we can watch TV all night long. It hurts so much we call it The Rack. But I'll take The Rack any day so I can watch TV all night long.

The rest of the family shows up from the airplane and now our vacation can really start!

Brenda is happy to see me. The big kids don't seem to care so much. I try to tell them about Mister Old Guy, but they just tell me I talk too much. Then they laugh at me because they think I am a baby who can't go on an airplane.

"Listen! I can too go on an airplane. Mommy doesn't want to, and I love her so much. So I went on the train ride to take care of her and now I have a pen pal!"

I showed them.

We all settle in and after a good night's sleep we are going to go to the Magic Kingdom. I am so excited I can hardly sleep.

Why is it magical? Who lives in the kingdom? How is Mister Old Guy? Who is he having dinner with tonight without us?

The next morning, we all get our acts together and find a train called the Monorail to take us to the Magic Kingdom.

Let me stop right here and tell you something. The Monorail train is the COOLEST thing I have ever seen in my whole life.

We wait, all nine of us, behind the yellow line. The adults are in front, and my mom is holding my hand tight. Swish, zoom, the Monorail floats right up in front of us. It's so shiny and smooth. Then the doors open, on the other side, and people get off. This is weird. How can we get on if the doors are open on the other side but not our side?

"Dad, how are we going to get on?"

"Just wait. Here we go."

The other doors close and then our side opens. No wonder this is going to take us to the Magic Kingdom because there is already so much magic happening! Our whole group gets on board and us kids push each other for the seats. There are enough for all of us, but it's still fun to push my brother.

Then, we're off!

Please stand clear of the doors.

We are all sitting but thanks!

For the comfort of others, no smoking is allowed.

"Mom! No smoking!"

She gives me The Look.

The Voice tells us more things and Brenda and I are about to jump out of our skin we are so excited.

We had a good, long day and are on the Monorail again to go back to the hotel. I think the Monorail is my favorite ride in all the park! I really like It's a Small World and the Tiki Room a lot, but there is something about the Monorail…sometimes we are riding up high, and sometimes we are right along the ground. I don't know how they do it but it's something else.

Brenda and I love the Monorail so much that we take turns in each other's rooms playing Monorail in the closet. At first, we can get our brothers and my sister to play along with us. Once, our dads even got in. But mostly we just play Monorail by ourselves. We stand outside the sliding closet door.

Please stand behind the yellow line as you wait for the Monorail to arrive.

We stand together, holding hands as the pretend Monorail glides up.

"Brenda, it's here, it's here!"

The closet door opens smoothly, and we enter the Monorail/closet.

Please stand clear of the doors.

We scooch deeper into the closet.

For the comfort of others, no smoking is allowed.

We look at each other and giggle.

Please hold on to the handrails.

We get on our tippy toes and hold on to the bar at the top of the closet.

Brenda is so good at remembering all of the safety announcements. When we arrive at the Magic Kingdom, we step carefully onto the platform outside of the closet doors.

When it's time to put on our swimming suits and go to the pool or the beach Brenda and I beg to stay in our rooms so we can play more Monorail. We are too little to stay by ourselves and have to tag along with everyone else. But we promise our Monorail system that we will be back soon.

The beach at the hotel is our parents' favorite place. They get lots of fruity drinks with alcohol and they don't even care how much pop us kids drink. It's paradise! Sue is the only one who doesn't drink pop though and she always wants to order chocolate milk. Even at the beach! She is so weird.

One day at the beach, a speed boat starts to zoom by and guess who is water skiing off the back of that boat? It's Goofy! He is so funny!! He is in a striped, old-timer bathing suit. Brenda and I can't stop laughing at how funny that guy is. The adults order more drinks because they can't believe their eyes.

On my birthday, our families go to a dress-up restaurant for dinner. It's our fanciest dinner of the trip. I think it's because I am turning six years old. My brother said I'm dumb and it's because it was the only night we could get a reservation. I don't know what that means but I know that I am NOT dumb and my brother most certainly is.

The tables are set with candles and there is a live band playing music on a stage in the corner. I ask my dad what it means to be a live band.

"I mean, aren't all band people alive? What is the other kind of band—a dead band?"

My sister rolls her eyes, and my dad laughs out loud. I don't know why he's laughing but it feels good to make him laugh.

We eat a fancy dinner and then at dessert time, I see our waitress and she is carrying a great big cake with candles on it. She is walking towards me and has a big smile on her face. How did she know it was my birthday? This is incredible! Then she looks at the alive band and the singer starts to sing Happy Birthday... to ME! The whole restaurant starts singing with them. I can't believe it. I am smiling so big that my face hurts. I don't think I am breathing. The famous singer from the alive band is looking at me and everyone is looking at me and there is so much singing. All for me. Because I am six and I am on a real vacation in Disney World. I am a lucky girl.

After my birthday, it's time to head back to home. Vacation is over. The airplane people go to the airport and Mom and I go to the train station in another taxicab.

We get to our sleeping room and Mom has had it. She needs a nap. By now I am a pro at the train riding, so I walk myself to the restaurant car and look for Mister Old Guy. He's not there. I'm a little bit sad because I want to tell him about my vacation and my birthday. I have some tears because he's my friend and I thought he'd be here. A worker lady sees me and asks me where my mom is. Then she helps me find my way back to our room place. Mom is NOT happy when I get back. I didn't know I wasn't supposed to leave the room. She sets me up to work on finishing my kindergarten homework packet, lights up another cigarette, and says she needs quiet so she can think and rest.

Later that day, a worker knocks on our door.

"I'm sorry ladies, but the dining car has broken down and is no longer functional. I can provide you with a couple of snacks here from this cart to tide you over."

Mom is nervous about this because we still have a long way to go. She says it will be a special new adventure and we will ration our food like the pioneers used to do in the old-timey days.

Did I tell you that the pull-down-from-the-ceiling-bed was out of the question and on both the going to vacation and the going home I had to share the little bed with my mommy? That made me both sad and angry because I was sure big enough for that bed and I didn't believe it would swallow me up and shoot me out somewhere over Godforsaken Kentucky or somewhere.

Well, the last night of our trip, we were hungry. Our snacks were gone, and we'd be home the next day. I was pretty hungry, but Mom said I had to be strong and if the pioneers could do it, so could I. So, I went to sleep and mom was going to stay up for a little bit to read her book. I snuggled in tightly between her and the cold wall and fell asleep to my growling tummy.

Even though I was sleeping, I felt something soft falling onto my face. I carefully opened one eye and looked up to see my mom holding a little bag of potato chips and eating them all herself! I sat up quick as I pushed off her body and then bounced off the wall.

"MOM! YOU SAID WE DIDN'T HAVE ANY FOOD LEFT AND THOSE CHIP CRUMBS ARE FALLING ON MY SLEEPING FACE!!!"

She finished chewing and reached the almost empty bag of Lay's out to me.

"Oh. Um, I found these after you fell asleep. I was going to save some for you. Look, there is one chip left, just for you!"

I gave her The Look as I grabbed the bag and gobbled up the last potato chip. Stinky mom. Potato chips are her favorite.

MOXIE MATTERS

1st Grade
1976-1977

With the frustrations of kindergarten behind me, I am ready for all that first grade has to offer. The elementary school gods smile upon me, and I am placed in the legendary Mr. Ashforth's class. Mr. Ashforth is tall and thin, with long brown feathered hair and frameless glasses that would darken in the sunlight. He is married with two sons (how lucky are they?) and drives an orange Volkswagen Bug. My brother had him and every parent in the neighborhood clamors for their child to be placed in his class.

The first day of first grade is one of the best days of my life. I'll start with the classroom. It is huge. Within the classroom itself are two, two-story clubhouse-type houses. Inside each, instead of chairs, there are vinyl car seat benches. Actual pieces of cars that we can sit on and read books. How did he make this magical thing happen? What kind of wizard is he? Besides seating, each of the four clubhouse rooms has shelves of books.

Each of those magical rooms is a different level that we kids get to earn the right to visit, based on our reading and maybe some other things. I want to spend all of my first-grade minutes in these cool spaces. For this reason alone—inside clubhouses with books everywhere—I love first grade.

Kindergarten was rough for me, and I got in trouble a few times. I don't want Mr. Ashforth to think I am naughty, but one day, I get in some trouble. I cannot help it that I like to make my friends laugh.

I am giggling and whispering to Jennifer Campbell. Suddenly, behind me comes a booming voice.

"Miss Modder!"

That is it. That is enough. I am ashamed of my behavior and blink back my tears. I will not break another rule in this wonderful man's classroom, or in any others for as long as I live.

First grade has a lot of exciting things and now it is my turn for the wonder that is Show-and-Tell. I wake up in the morning and carefully search my bedroom. I know immediately what I will bring and carefully tuck it under my arm. After my same breakfast of Skippy peanut butter and strawberry jelly on a single piece of Holsum white bread (cut in two rectangular pieces) with a glass of Orange Hi-C (the elixir of the gods), I set out to walk to the end of my block where Hatch Elementary stands in all its glory.

At the end of Lenox St. is the very busy Ridgeland Ave, and to get to school, we have to cross. There to lead us to safety, every day of my elementary school career is the legend herself...Frosty.

Every child in the neighborhood knows and loves Frosty. Even the kids who live on the other side of the school will find it their honor to walk home with a friend on our side, just to be crossed by the loving, smiling, wonderful woman we all know only as "Frosty." She is always in a full crossing guard uniform that includes a coat and hat for absolutely any kind of weather. My favorite is her winter gear where only her smooth pink face can be seen.

To me, Frosty is a very old woman with white hair, a thick body, the whitest skin with perpetually pink cheeks, and twinkly blue eyes. She knows all of our names, gives hugs, and occasionally some kind of candy treat. She rules that corner with the sweetest demeanor and no child ever, ever disobeys her. I love her and get to see her four times a day, five days a week.

Our school day starts at 9:00 am. We all go home for lunch from 12-1:00, and then school ends at 3:30, 3:00 on Wednesdays for a teacher meeting. I treasure my moments at the corner with Frosty and feel extra close to her for two reasons. One, her corner is at the end of MY block. Two, she lives near my grandparents in a town not too far away. I don't know how my parents got this information, but it makes her feel like my very own grandma.

Back to first grade and Show-and-Tell. I carefully tuck my Shawn Cassidy album under my arm and start my block-long walk to school. After showing Frosty my treasure, I cross the street and head straight to Mr. Ashforth whom I see standing in the middle of the playground. I am so excited to show him what I brought to share. But something terrifying happens as I approach him. I hear a screech and then someone screams, "Shawn Cassidy, oh my God I love him!!!" More screeches. I stop, drop my book bag, and cling to my album. It is then that I realize girls all over the playground have spotted me and start running towards me. I make eye contact with Mr. Ashforth and he mouths, "RUN!"

I run. And I am chased by gobs of screaming elementary school girls who are so in love with the hunk that is Shawn Cassidy that they act like complete maniacs. What will they do if they catch me? There is no way I am going to let that happen. I zip all around the playground with a pack of rabid girls behind me and a whole lot of confused kids stopping and staring at the sight.

Finally, a whistle blows several times and a larger-than-life voice booms.

"ENOUGH!"

All action freezes as everyone turns to stare at my hero, Mr. Ashforth. He motions for me to come to him. With a wink and a smile from my teacher, I gladly hand over my prized possession which he keeps safe until Show-and-Tell later.

I love first grade!

I think Joe Hernandez is beautiful and I think I should give him a kiss to show him how I feel. His hair. Joe Hernandez has the tallest, most gorgeous afro I have ever seen. It is kiss-worthy for sure. I guess he isn't too keen on me kissing him because as soon as I tell him my plans, he takes off running.

I am in hot pursuit, and it doesn't take long for me to reach out my hands and grab hold of that beautiful hair and jerk him to a stop. By his hair. He has a look of pain and terror as I pull his face back and plant one right on his lips. Then I release my grip, and he is off running again. This time I don't run after him. I am really sad that he runs. Mr. Ashforth is striding towards me with pursed lips and a scrunched-up face. I have to sit on the wall for the rest of recess.

It is time for winter break. It is that two-week time when Santa comes, and I'll play outside in the snow all day if I can. One day, the doorbell rings and that is always an exciting thing.

Company!

Mom is confused and maybe a little annoyed as we aren't expecting anyone. I don't leave my spot on the family room couch where I am watching cartoons. My mom yells my name from the front of the house.

"Karen! You have a guest!"

What? I have a guest? I go racing through the kitchen, dining room, and stop in my tracks, see my guest, and run to my bedroom where I dive into my bed and under my covers.

Dad shows up and half-drags me back out as the adults are all chuckling. My guest is none other than my favorite teacher… Mr. Ashforth! And he brought his two sons with him. They are around my age and all three of them are standing in my house. MY HOUSE! Ack! I am weirdly excited and don't know what to do. How is my teacher in my house? It turns out, every year, he visits all his students at home during the winter break. Every year, all his students. He chats with my parents and me for a bit and then they are on their way. Dad tells me when he visited my brother at home, four years ago, my brother hid from him the entire time.

2nd Grade
1977-1978

I can't remember exactly when I find out that Ms. Nelson is going to be my second-grade teacher, but I know I am very happy. She is young and where Mr. Ashforth is very tall, Ms. Nelson is tiny. I feel like she is just a little taller than I am.

Ms. Nelson insists that we call her "Ms" and my mom likes her spunk. She drives a small, bright blue, MG Midget convertible. Her hair is dark brown and cut short. She has a full face of make-up that always includes a bright-colored lipstick. I think she is all kinds of wonderful.

Our class is what our district is calling a pod. Half of our class will be second graders and the other half are third graders. I feel lucky to be chosen to be in a class with the 'big' kids and it honestly adds a whole other layer of excitement for me.

I am in second grade. There is nothing I can't do. Ms. Nelson always tells me I can do anything, and I believe her!

One day, Ms. Nelson tells our class that we will be hosting a circus for the rest of the school. A CIRCUS! I love to put on a show, and this seems like it's really going to be quite a show. I've got plans for this circus. I quickly walk to her desk.

"Excuse me, Ms. Nelson?"

"Yes, Karen?"

She listens with her big, lipstick smile.

"Would you like me to stay after school today so we can talk about how to do this circus? I have a lot of ideas."

"Karen, I appreciate your big ideas. How about I do the big planning and you can be a special part of the circus, just like all the kids in the class?

She winks at me. I try to wink back but I think it's a double-eye blink.

"Well that is a very good idea. You are the teacher so that makes sense."

"Why thank you."

"You're welcome! I put on a lot of shows on my front lawn. Can I do a lot of things in the circus?"

"Karen, you can do anything you can dream. Now head back to your desk so we can all work together to plan things."

"You got it!"

I try to wink again and head back to my desk. A circus. This is going to be fantastic.

Our class spends days and weeks planning all the acts, painting signs, and organizing the food that will be served—it is so magical to me. We take over the school auditorium and my whole class is buzzing with the thrill of being circus performers.

It's the big day, under the big top! All of the other classes in the whole school will take turns coming to the circus today. Our parents are invited too so they can see what all of our hard work was for.

I prep for my tight-walking routine, knowing I have a quick change before taking my turn at the fortune teller's table. Ms. Nelson worked extra hard to organize where every one of her kids needed to be and when we needed to be there. The big clock on the wall tells us when to be where. It's a good thing Ms. Nelson taught us how to tell time! The energy in the theater is full of excitement as we open the doors and welcome our guests.

Ms. Nelson is the best teacher ever. I love her and I think she really loves me back. She laughs at my jokes and gives me big hugs pretty much every time I make her laugh.

Hair Salon

"Karen! Let's go!"

My mom yells up the stairs to my bedroom.

"Okay Mom, coming!"

I carefully lift the needle off one of my most favorite things, my Free to Be You and Me album, and place it on the holder. Then I pick it up, so slowly, holding only the sides with the insides of my hands like my brother taught me. After slipping it into its paper protector, I slide it right into the bright pink cardboard album cover. Finally, I close the lid on my brand-new Mickey Mouse record player. Oh, I love it so! It is white and turquoise and even has a handle to carry it around the house, even the neighborhood if I want to, just like a cool suitcase.

Grabbing my windbreaker, I fly down the stairs to meet my mom. Today is one of my favorite days. I get to go with her to the hair salon! We meet at the back door. I grab her hand and look up with a huge smile on my face. Together we walk the few short blocks to her salon on North Avenue.

North Avenue is a magical place with all of the best stores on it. But it is a really busy street, so I can never go across by myself. Across the street is a neighborhood of the city of Chicago and a little girl has no business going there by herself. But North Avenue, on the Oak Park side, has our dentist, Frank's Candy Store, the beef sandwich place, the sub place, the Jewel, and my favorite… mom's hair salon.

I don't always get to come.

"Now remember, you sit quietly while I get my hair done."

"Okay Mom, don't you worry. I'll sit quietly and I'll sit still."

"Oh, I just bet you will."

I am not always good at sitting still or keeping quiet. But I love her hair guy. He is also the owner of the salon and I want to be invited back. I will try my hardest.

Walking in, I am giggling because I am so excited. It takes a minute to adjust my eyes because it is dark and very smoky. My mom lights up one of her Benson & Hedges with her new lighter and adds her own smoke to the foggy place.

I let my feet sink into the thick, shag, wall-to-wall dark orange carpet and make my way slowly over to one of the yellowy velvet couches. My mom taps me on my shoulder and hands me a shiny coin.

"Here you go. Get yourself a treat from the vending machine before you sit."

As her hair guy, a dead ringer for my grandma's favorite singer, Tony Orlando, steers my mom towards the hair-washing chairs, I am drawn to the light of the vending machine. I look at my choices, but I always pick the same thing…a bottle of orange pop.

Sliding in my coin, I press the number that matches my pick. Within seconds, an ice-cold bottle of pop drops down. I bend down and look up into the machine the best that I can. Where does it even come from? How does it stay so cold? I didn't care, I have what I came for. One of the worker ladies walks up with a bottle opener and pop goes the top.

Grabbing my drink, I take my seat on the couch. Orange pop in one hand, I use my other to rub the soft, velvet material. One direction smooths it out and makes it dark. The other direction lightens the color and stands the little fabric thingies up. It is sooo soft, my pop is cold, and I make myself comfy.

I watch and see Mom's hair guy is able to wash mom's hair with a lit cigarette passing between his mouth and his wet hands. He is so cool. His black feathered hair is just like Shawn Cassidy's, only darker. My dad has black hair but not much of it. He calls it bald. He also says God only created a few perfect heads and he put hair on the rest. Well, I have hair and so does Mom's hair guy. I notice he has a whole lot of hair so our heads must not be perfect.

"Mom? Mom!"

She pulls the little towel from over her ears.

"What?" She takes a puff on her new cigarette.

"Mom, if dad has a bald head and it's perfect, then what does his head look like under all that hair?"

He laughs out loud. Mom does not.

"Karen, remember it's your time to sit quietly and enjoy your treat."

"Got it Mom. Sorry, just wondering."

Then he gets to work on her head. She comes every single week so he can wash it and then set it in curlers. Once the curlers are in, she sits under the big warm dryer. Then he will "brush it out'" but he doesn't really.

One of the beautiful hair ladies gives her a magazine to read while she sits under the dryer. I see my opportunity for a chat.

"Hi Mom! Hi Mom!" I have to shout a little bit because the dryer is loud and covers her ears.

"Karen! I hear you just fine. What is it?"

"Nothing, I just wanted to say hi."

"Okay, hi dear. Can you go and grab my cigarettes and lighter from my purse?"

"Sure!"

I love to be a helper.

"And can you grab an ashtray from the counter?"

"Yep!" I squint my eyes as I walk around the place. Between the mix of all the different ladies smoking and the cans of hairspray shooting around, it is like walking through magical clouds in heaven.

After he is all done with the "brush out," he pulls that spray out from the bottom shelf of his hair shelves and starts the spraying. There is so much spraying. He sprays on the top, around the sides, up from the bottom, around the top again and then one last big blast for good measure. Mom says this is to make sure her hair doesn't move until she comes in again next week. It works too!

Mom pays and hair guy tells me I did a great job and can come back whenever I want.

"Well thanks but I am pretty sure I only get to come when no one is home to look out for me. It stinks to be the youngest sometimes. But thanks for letting me watch and drink your orange pop!"

Mom grabs my hand after lighting up another Benson & Hedges. She really likes those things. She pulls open the door and we have to stop for a minute to let our eyes adjust to the bright sunshine on North Avenue. A pouf of smoke/hairspray follows us right out the door as we breathe in the outside air. I look up at my beautiful mom with her fresh hair-do.

"Thanks Mom. I love it in there!"

Hand in hand, we walk the few blocks back home.

Walking to Church

I'm holding Mommy's hand as we walk to church. It's a Lutheran church, at the other end of our block. Right across the street from church is my school! We can walk there without even crossing the street! I love church. I mostly love holding Mommy or Daddy's hand while we walk. We go out of our back door, down the back stairs, and through our backyard to the Secret Shortcut.

Daddy and Mr. Tanner, who lives behind us, put their money together to hire a guy to put a sidewalk made of cement down on the ground where our garages back up to each other. It's just the right size to hold all of our garbage cans and it's even big enough to ride a bike through, one kid at a time.

The Tanner's and Smith's driveways are right next to each other. When we take the Secret Shortcut we are careful not to walk on the Smith's driveway. The Smiths are really nice people, but Mr. Smith wouldn't put his money in for the Secret Shortcut, so we are careful to walk on the Tanner driveway only. Dad says we have to prove a point. The Smiths have a new metal swing set in their backyard though, and I wish we didn't have to prove a point because then I could take a quick swing on our way to church.

At the bottom of the driveway, we turn right and pass by different houses of people who are friends, and people who we don't know. Then, after a couple of minutes, we are at church! We walk every single Sunday. Even if it's raining. Even if it's snowing. We never drive. Ever. Today is sunny and springtime. I can smell lilac flowers and the big trees over my head are filling up with leaves. It smells like it might rain later today so we have our umbrellas just in case. Mine is a bubble umbrella! It's clear—that means you can see right through it—and is it like half of a bubble that starts over my head and then comes down, all around me, past my shoulders! It is just about the coolest umbrella a girl can have.

I feel special walking to church. A lot of our neighbors, well, almost all of our neighbors, are Catholics and they walk in the other direction to go to their church. They have to walk a bunch of blocks and cross a lot of streets. But that's what Catholics do I guess.

Once we get to church, we go right in and sit in our spot—second pew on the left, aisle side. Mom and Dad smile at people and after the big bells ring, the loud organ plays, and then Pastor starts to talk. Soon we stand up and share the peace with the people around us. I flash a peace sign with my fingers and Mommy gives me a gentle elbow which reminds me I'm supposed to shake people's hands.

Then, we settle in for the rest of the service. I snuggle right into Mommy's side. She has such a pretty singing voice and she's squishy and warm to cuddle up to. I once told her she was squishy and warm and that did not go over well. I think squishy is nice when you're a Mommy.

I always like to cuddle up to Mommy at church because it's a whole hour of quiet time and being close to her. She is pretty and funny. My mommy laughs a lot, and her friends tell me that I am lucky because she is so funny. She puts on a whole face of make-up with lotions and powders and creams that make her a different kind of pretty, but she really likes to do it. Every morning, she does a lot of spritzes of Estée Lauder's Youth Dew perfume. Then she smells delicious! I can smell her from across the room sometimes.

When church is over, the kids run up the stairs to our Sunday School classes while the adults go into the Fellowship Hall for visiting, coffee, and sometimes, on a special occasion they will have a guest speaker and they call that a Forum. No kids are allowed.

On this day, there is a Forum for the adults. The kids are all told to stop on the second floor in the gym for a special time. My brother and sister are nowhere to be found, so I park my fanny on the gym floor and look around at all of the other kids while the grown-ups do some talking at us. When the talking stops, they tell us we are dismissed.

That means we can go.

I am happy it's over and head down the stairs to find my parents. If the talker in the Forum is still talking, the kids wait outside the closed doors. No other kids are around so I do a little jump up and see through the window on the door that the talker is talking, and the adults are sitting. They look serious and like it might take a while. I decide to walk myself home.

I know the way! I pick up my umbrella and head out the side door, take a left at the bottom of the sidewalk, and decide I'm going to gallop all the way to the Tanner's driveway. I make it exactly three houses when it starts to drizzle. I put up my bubble umbrella and decide to walk so I don't slip on the wet sidewalk. I love the smell of rain and how the raindrops make the sidewalk darker when they hit the ground. I'm two houses away from the Tanner's when I decide to skip the rest of the way.

I made it! I'm alone so I look left, then right, and then I do something crazy. I walk on the Smith's side of the driveway, all the way up to the Shortcut. No one even sees me! Plus, the Smith's station wagon isn't in their driveway, and I think they are at the Baptist church that you need a car to get to. Too bad I can't swing because the rain is a little heavier.

I get to our backyard, up the back stairs, onto the porch, and set my wet and open umbrella down to dry out like Mommy taught me to. I go to open the back door. It's locked. But that can't be! David and Susan have to be in front of me and home first. They have a key because they are older than ten and almost grown-ups. I try the door again. It is still locked.

Tears start coming out of my eyes and I feel scared.

Think Karen Melissa, think.

I jump up to look through the window and the kitchen is dark. The rain is coming down even harder. My tears are coming down just as hard. Where are my brother and sister? I bang on the door so they can hear me. I know Mommy and Daddy are still at church with the talker guy. But Sunday School lady said, "You are dismissed." That means we can go home. So I did. By myself! I did it!

I am really scared and sit down on the porch floor. It's dirty and I'm in my dress and tights. Now there is thunder. I grab my umbrella and run down the stairs, through the yard, zig-zag through the Shortcut, and down the Tanner's side of the double driveway.

"I'M SORRY GOD! I WENT ON THE WRONG SIDE AND NOW MY BROTHER AND SISTER ARE DISAPPEARED! I'M SORRY!"

My umbrella handle is slippery as I run through what is now pouring rain. I jump over any big puddles and keep going. Mommy and Daddy are at church. They are at church, and I am almost there.

I make it. I pull the heavy wood door open all by myself and step inside. I shake out my umbrella with my shaky hands and snuffle all the crying snot back into my nose the best I can. Nobody is around and now I am really scared. I tiptoe over to the Fellowship Hall door and jump up to see what's inside. Talker guy is still talking, and all the parents are still listening.

What is going on? Where are all the kids? Did they get kidnapped like in Chitty Chitty Bang Bang? Are they all in cages somewhere? Should I have come back? Yes! Yes, I will rescue all of the kids.

I take a deep breath and wipe the back of my arm to catch the last of my crying nose drips. I walk over to the stairs and hold the railing tight while I start to walk up. It's so quiet and I go onto my tippy toes so the bad guys won't hear me coming. I get to the second floor and look through the glass door to Pastors office.

Lights off, empty. I take giant steps over to the gym and the lights are off there too.

This isn't looking good for all of the kids in my church. Should I go downstairs, throw open the doors, and tell everyone their kids have been kidnapped by the scary guy from Chitty Chitty Bang Bang? Or do I keep going up to the third floor, where all of the Sunday School classrooms are? I am feeling very brave all of a sudden, so I hug the wall and hold that railing very tightly while I sneak up the stairs.

I hear sounds as I get closer. When I get to the top, I turn the corner and am face-to-face with…

Mrs. Draper.

"Karen Modder! What are you doing? Why aren't you in your classroom??"

"I, um, I…Where are the kids?"

"What do you mean?"

"Where are all of the kids? Are they in cages?"

"What on earth young lady? Why would you say that? The kids are all in their classrooms with their teachers where you are supposed to be."

"But in the gym, after the talking, they said 'You are dismissed.' That means we are done, and we can go home."

Tears start to come into my eyeballs again. Mrs. Draper comes closer and kneels down in front of me. I feel scared again.

"I thought it was done. I went home. But the back door was locked, and it was raining and there was thunder, and I was scared. So I got brave and came back and I figured since no kids were waiting for their parents then the Chitty Chitty Bang Bang guy must have taken them all and, and put them in cages."

Mrs. Draper holds both of my hands.

"No honey. The kids were dismissed to come up to their Sunday School classes. But aren't you brave for going all the way home and so smart for coming all the way back."

"Thank you. I was proud and then I was scared and then I was brave. I was going to rescue all of the kids!"

"Well dear, Sunday School is over in just a couple of minutes. Why don't we wait here for your brother and sister to come by."

"Am I in trouble? Did I play hooky? I sure didn't do it on purpose."

More tears and I just cannot make them stop.

"Oh no, you made a mistake. Then you did the right thing. I'll tell your teacher what happened."

"Thank you. I really would have rescued all the kids you know."

"Oh, I am sure you would have. You're really something else."

"Thank you, I know."

End of Summer 1978

"Karen, sit down, we've got something to talk to you about."

I thought for sure Mrs. Jablonski across the street called my parents to tell them that Katherine, Mary, and I were caught red-handed playing in all the treasures in their basement. After a full day of exploring the rows and rows of tagged items for the glorious flea market that Mr. Jablonski spends all of weekend time at, he came down the basement steps that evening and there we were, in full dress up, laden with jewels, mouths hanging open when he yelled out our names.

Mary and I dropped our frocks, threw off our hats, and not-so-carefully clunked all the jewels to the floor and ran out of that house as fast as we could to the safety of our own. It was close, but he didn't catch us. That's why I thought for sure Mom and Dad called me down to the kitchen. Even though Katherine's mom said we could play down there, her dad forbade it and we got caught. I skulk out of my room and turn the corner to the kitchen, head down.

"Have a seat. We've got something to talk to you about."

Before they can get a punishment in, I say, "Mrs. J said we could play down there, we didn't think it was bad to do it!"

"What? No, it's nothing like that. We got a letter here from the school."

"But school hasn't started yet."

I am confused.

"There's a new program starting this year called PROBE. Your scores last year, plus Ms. Nelson's recommendation, have qualified for you to participate. It's for gifted kids."

"Well, I love Ms. Nelson and I love school, so it sounds like it's a good thing?"

"Yes, it is a good thing. We are happy to have you participate. But the letter says you'll be the only third grader at Hatch, well, the only third grader in the whole district, who will participate. Is that okay?"

"What does it mean?"

I am excited and nervous all put together.

"It looks like you'll go to third grade in the mornings and then after lunch, when you go back to school, you'll be in the PROBE classroom with the other kids. They will be kids who also had high achievement test scores and whose teachers thought they would do well in the program. But you'll be in that class with kids of all ages—4th, 5th, and 6th. You'll all learn together. What do you think?"

"Cool! Yes! Who's the teacher?"

"Mrs. Bennett, the 6th grade teacher."

"The one everyone loves? Yes, yes, yes!"

Mommy!

Sometimes Mommy likes to be silly and call me Mommy.

"Mommy! Mommy! Come quick!"

I can't stop smiling as I run towards my mom's voice. I run down the stairs and towards the kitchen.

"Mommy! Come quick!"

I see she's not in the kitchen, so I head towards my parent's bedroom. Jackpot!

"Hi honey! What do you need?"

"Mommy, I need some snuggles!"

Oh good, my favorite! I crawl in next to my mom in her big, cozy bed. The lights are off and the TV is glowing one of the black and white movies she likes to watch. I love to cuddle up with my mommy and think she's so silly when she calls me mommy.

Sometimes she calls me and needs me to get her something from the kitchen. Usually a cold bottle of Tab or some chips. But the best times, the very best are when she wants cuddles. So I always stop what I am doing and run to find her.

We have two TVs in our house. One in the TV room by the kitchen, and one in my parents' room. Mommy is in here a lot. Pretty much all afternoon and all night. If she's taking a nap, we all know to be really, super quiet, and don't come in her room. She takes a nap every day.

On the weekends especially, she watches movies during the day. Sometimes she is sitting up and I snuggle into the crook of her right arm. Sometimes, she is lying down and we snuggle up close. Esther Williams and her swimming movies are her real favorite. She also loves Fred Astaire, Ginger Rogers, and their dancing movies. Those are my favorites! Sometimes it's the scary Alfred Hitchcock movies. I like those too.

The big bed takes up most of the room. In front of it is her dresser with a beautiful, mirrored tray loaded with perfumes and pretty things. Estée Lauder is her favorite, Youth Dew the preferred scent. Every year my dad buys her some and I give her a big make-up gift that comes when you buy the perfume. She loves it.

She loves to sit on the edge of her bed, TV on, ashtray nearby, and get beautiful with her make-up and perfumes. I love to watch her.

MEDIUM

LOW · HIGH

MOXIE METER

Putting On A Show

The sun is just beginning to rise as I hear footsteps coming up the driveway. I unfurl from my sleeping bag and slowly sit up. The darkness covers me as I sit tall, suppressing my energy as the footsteps begin to ascend the back stairs to our porch. With the creak of the screen door, a hand reaches in to slowly lift the lid off our milk box.

"Good mornin,' Good mornin,' It's great to stay up late. Good mornin,' Good mornin,' to you!"

The milkman almost tumbles backward down the stairs as I sing my greeting to him. He rights himself and looks right at me, shaking his head. I look right back waiting for his reply. It never comes. Just the shake of his head as he delivers our two percent and walks back to his truck.

But that doesn't matter to me. Not one bit. Putting on a show, any kind of show is in my DNA, and I have been performing for all kinds of audiences my entire life.

I especially like to produce, direct, and star in my one-woman show, performed on our front lawn. This stage meets all of my needs, not too big and not too small. Somewhere between a square and a rectangle, it is just right.

The lawn is so small that our lawnmower is electric. Once one of the Modder children turns twelve years old, they are old enough to use the electric mower. This is a big task because if the mower is to accidentally mow over the bright orange extension cord, the brave family member would be electrocuted and dead. I often sit in the front window, safely tucked inside the house to watch my dad and my older brother as they take on the dangerous chore.

At the top of our lawn nearest the house stands a hedge of evergreens my dad keeps trimmed to about three feet high. There is just enough space behind the hedge, and in front of the house, for a backstage changing area. Each summer, in front of the hedge, my dad tends to carefully chosen annual flowers. Golden yellow and orange marigolds are my favorite and create a beautifully fragrant backdrop for my shows.

On show day, I wander my house and gather a variety of costumes, including but not limited to elastic banded skirts (which could be worn as either a skirt, or a strapless dress depending on what the act called for), headbands, wigs, vests, boots, shoes, and handbags, and I place them "backstage" (behind the evergreen hedge).

My costumes inspire my performances. The blonde wig I find on the floor of my mom's bedroom closet makes for a Mae West skit where I stuff my chest with rolled socks and tell my audience to "Come up and see me sometime." A long skirt and plain blouse transforms me into Laura Ingalls Wilder as I act out a scene from Little House on the Prairie. Perhaps my favorite skit to perform is anything Love Boat related. A thin ribbon tied loosely in a bow around my neck, and I become Julie McCoy, Cruise Director extraordinaire. There are endless possibilities and ideas flow from one show to the next.

Next comes my marketing plan, or what I call, "Go and grab an audience." I work the top half of our block and knock on the doors of our immediate neighbors. For anyone brave enough to answer (knowing full well what my ask will be), I invite them to my show. For the low-ticket price of a single quarter, they can bring their lawn chair to the sidewalk and enjoy my latest performance. That's right, audience members bring their own seats. I see the importance of comfort and want everyone to have their favorite chair as they enjoy my show.

I absolutely sell out my first performance. In fact, for some it is standing room only. They line up on the parkway, behind the seated guests. Then, as the summer drags on and interest in the performing arts drops off with family and friends, I know I can always count on Mrs. O'Rourke from two doors down.

Without fail, when I hit the O'Rourke driveway, I get a spring in my step. As I bounce up the five cement stairs to their front door, I can't help but smile. Mrs. O'Rourke will likely be in a whirlwind of activity at her house. If any other family members open the door after I ring the bell, they simply call out, "Ma! Karen's back!"

If she opens the door herself, a big smile forms, "Oh Karen, I hoped it was you! Hold on, hon!" She pauses whatever she is doing, and grabs her lawn chair from her garage, quarter in hand.

Once I snag Mrs. O'Rourke, the show can go on! As I lead her to front row seating, she might yell out to any neighbor she can see to join the show. She even offers to pay for their ticket! I think that worked once.

Show time. There are four kinds of acts I perform: singing, dancing, joke telling, and skit performing. Some shows include all four, some just one. It all depends on my creative mood at the time.

I'd like to thank Mrs. O'Rourke for being a season ticket holder and closing each show with a standing ovation. I'd also like to thank Mrs. Adelmen, my older-than-dirt next-door neighbor for often rapping on her front room window to remind me not to accidentally step on her driveway.

Many thanks pour out to the surrounding neighbors including the mean Mr. and Mrs. Johnson on the other side of us who refuse to even answer the door but let me know of their disinterest by shouting at me right through the paned glass. I simply couldn't have pulled off the productions I did if the Motts, Jablonskis, Madisons, and Bandinos wouldn't have paused their lawn mowing when they saw a masterpiece underway on my lawn stage.

Weather easily contributes to the availability of shows and what I offer. Thankfully, the front lawn is only one of my many performance venues. The absolute best stage for me is the front room of any extended family members at the family party. When the family gathers, for absolutely any reason, I put on a show. At some point, usually after dinner, my two cousins and I start the planning.

To be completely honest, I'm pretty sure I tell them a show is brewing and then I tell them what their roles will be. I then very generously direct them as backup dancers for me, accompanists for me, or supporting actors in a skit I have written in my mind.

As plans begin to be set in motion, it becomes time to survey the house for costumes and props. My signature costume looks flow from the elastic banded skirts, many of which my mom sewed for me herself. As previously mentioned, these skirts can be utilized as skirts (boring), strapless gowns (now you're talking), and yes, even headpieces! The headpieces were introduced to me by my artistic older cousin. A skirt-wig gives huge creative energy to a production.

If the show has a musical undertone, instruments can be found in a variety of places including the bottom of bedroom closets, basement shelves, attics, and even garages. Harmonicas and castanets always add a little extra zip to our acts.

Family Show showtime always occurs after a meal and hours before anyone thinks of departing the scene. My parents, aunts, and uncles respond best after the consumption of martinis, manhattans, beer, and occasionally wine. My grandparents endure the shows and Grandma Modder may be the only one to crack a smile at any point. I love performing, especially when people laugh. Making anyone laugh feels like I am a bottle of pop—full of bubbly energy inside that explodes when opened and poured out. I love that feeling as much as I love opening a cold bottle of Pepsi.

3rd Grade
1978-1979

Third grade starts and I have a very big spring in my step. I have Mr. Martin. He is quiet, always wears a tie, and doesn't at all like the PROBE program. Every morning from the time school starts at 9 a.m., until noon, I'll be in his class. Then I go home for lunch from 12-1:00 and the rest of the afternoon (1-3:30) is spent in glorious Probe with the most incredible Mrs. Bennett as our teacher.

Everyone treats me special and even Mr. Donaldson is proud that the only third grader in the district comes from his school. There is even a newspaper article written about us and my name is in it as the only third grader. My parents are happy about that. Ms. Nelson even finds me once in my classroom and tells me how proud she is of me and that she expects great things. I will never disappoint Ms. Nelson, not ever.

Crabby Mr. Martin tries to make me feel bad about leaving his room every day, but I can't get to Mrs. Bennett and PROBE fast enough. Our classroom is on the third floor—with all the big 5th and 6th graders! I have my own hook and cubby in the classroom and the bigger kids are all nice to me. I think each one of them is so smart and am glad to sit with them at tables, not desks, in our PROBE room.

The days are getting cooler as fall has officially begun. Third grade is off to a great start. My homework is done, and I grab my powder-blue windbreaker as I run out the back door.

"Mom! I'm going to go see if Thomas can play!"

Thomas O'Neill:
- ☑ Best friend
- ☑ Husband in an unofficial ceremony officiated by my sister the summer before Thomas and I started kindergarten
- ☑ Jonathan to my Jennifer Hart
- ☑ Bosley to my Sabrina Duncan
- ☑ Partner in attempted crime...

My mom is in her room watching TV.

"Okay, be back when the streetlights come on!"

As I get to the middle of my driveway, I have a big decision to make: run across the lawns or play it safe and take the sidewalk? Am I feeling lucky? Four houses separate us with the first being Mr. and Mrs. Johnson. She always wears a dress and lipstick, and he is tall and frowny, white hair slicked back from his angry face. No one, I mean NO ONE is allowed to touch a single blade of grass on their lawn. I can always charm a smile out of Mrs. Johnson if she is alone. But not Mr. Johnson. No way. He often sits on a chair inside the front room window and stares out at us kids. If a ball rolls onto their lawn, you can just kiss that ball goodbye. The exception is if you know they aren't home.

On this fine fall day, I peek in their side garage window as I skip past. No car. Dare I dash across the yards, getting me to Thomas's house that much quicker?

Yes. I feel lucky.

I look left, look right, and run as fast as I can across their yard. I stop at the next driveway and hold my breath. I did it! No mean old Mr. Johnson yelling at me! This is my lucky day.

The next house is empty because the Francos moved out last week, so it is an easy decision to run across their front yard. One house to go...the Dulch's. Mrs. Dulch looks like she could be twins with the wicked witch from The Wizard of Oz. She has black hair and a hooked nose. And why did they have rhyming names? NOT a coincidence in my book. Her daughter, Stephanie, is just a year older than Thomas and me, but she thinks she is better than us, so we never play together. My mom says they are "stuck up." I'm not sure what that means but I steer clear of Stephanie Dulch. Because it is my lucky day, I go ahead and run right on their stuck-up lawn.

I make it to Thomas's and knock on the back door. Mrs. O'Neill answers, and she is one of my favorite people. She always has a great, big smile and a hug for me. I think because she has four boys, she thinks girls are pretty great. Plus, I was born on St. Patrick's Day and her name is Patricia, so we have a special connection in her eyes.

"Karen, darling, come in! How are you, love? Sit down, sit down. Oh, it's so good to see you dear!"

Mrs. O'Neill really likes it when I come over. She smells like Dove soap and happiness to me. I could sit with her all day.

"Mrs. O'Neill, is Thomas home? Can he play?"

"Oh sure, dear. Thomas! Your girlfriend Karen is here!"

Thomas appears in the kitchen doorway, his hair tousled and a little too long.

"Maaaahm! She is NOT my girlfriend."

"Yeah, I'm his WIFE!"

Thomas turns a splotchy bright red all over his neck and face as I grab his hand and head out the door.

"Bye Mrs. O'Neill! He'll be home when the streetlights come on!"

"Good-bye my darlings! Come back soon honey!"

Thomas tries to give me a dirty look as we reach his backyard. But I stick out my tongue and do my best single-eye-cross-eyed face and he bursts into giggles. We drop hands and as we walk slowly down his driveway, I share my thoughts for the day.

"Look, Thomas, I am having a very lucky day. I know that we usually fight crime, but what do you say to maaaybeee doing one?"

He gives me a serious side-eye, but I continue.

"Hear me out."

I point at the empty house two doors down.

"The Franco's moved out forever ago and no one has moved in. I'm pretty sure that means the house is going to stay empty. I'm pretty sure that means we need to somehow get inside and consider making it our new fort. What do you think?"

Thomas thinks for a minute.

"Well, I think we've solved enough crimes that we should be able to figure out how. Let's walk over there and look around. But we need to be careful and act like nothing is up."

He is so smart. We casually stroll down the sidewalk and right up the driveway. We even whistle a little tune to look very relaxed. The front door is on the side of this house, and it has five steps leading up to it. We sit carefully on the second step, then slowly, carefully slide our bottoms up each step until we are sitting at the top. We turn to face each other.

"Thomas, look, there is a mail slot on the door. If we can somehow get our hand up in there, we can unlock the door and then just walk right in. We could be having important meetings in there TONIGHT."

I start to stand. Thomas pulls me back down.

He scream-whispers at me, "Wait. We don't know what kind of lock we're dealing with. We need to hold open that mail slot and use a mirror to see exactly what lock they've got on this place."

"Good thinking! I've got a mirror in my room. Let's go!"

Just as we stand to go to my house, the Johnson's car creeps past the house. Mr. Johnson hits the brakes and leans over his wife as he rolls her window down.

"What are you kids up to? Get away from there!"

He inches forward and hits the brakes again, causing Mrs. Johnson's hat to fall over her eyes.

"And stay off my lawn!!"

He cruises to their driveway and parks his car as we walk on the sidewalk, heads down, to my house.

Thomas is a little sweaty.

"Oh boy, the jig is up. He knows. We can't get in there now."

"Thomas, listen to me, it will be fine. Let's play in my basement for a little while, let things settle here, and then go back with my mirror. We can do this. Think how GREAT it will be to have a whole house for a fort!"

"Okay, okay, you're right. You're always right!"

Instead of playing, we share a cold bottle of Pepsi and eat some Jay's potato chips. I feel enough time has passed and go upstairs to get my mirror. Oh, how I love my mirror. It is light pink plastic with a solid handle. There is a mirror on one side and when I flip it over, it is the back of a girl's head with two yellow, yarn braids coming down the back. It looks just like the back of my head, and it is all mine—not passed down from my older sister. It is a true treasure, and I am proud to use it on this lucky, lucky day of mine to help us get into the empty house, our future headquarters for all things fun!

We decide to whistle-slow-walk back to the Franco's empty house and get no angry eyes from Mr. Johnson. My lucky streak continues! Once we get to the top of the stairs, Thomas thinks I should be the lookout while he jimmies the mirror through the slot to position it just-so and get a look at the kind of lock we will then need to open by putting our arm through the mail slot. Top-notch plan from my best friend/husband.

Until
everything
goes
wrong.

While I look out towards the street, Thomas opens the mail slot. He snakes the mirror up, but his hand is a little pudgy and won't go through the slot while he holds the mirror. I hear the horrible sound of plastic hitting linoleum and round on Thomas as he stands…staring at his now empty hand.

"Thomas! My mirror! Where is my mirror?"

"Jesus, Mary, and Joseph. I dropped it. I dropped the mirror!"

"Thomas NOOOOO! We've got to get it back. That's my special mirror. It looks just like me."

Tears fill my eyes, and I can't see. I love that mirror with everything in my being. I have to be brave. It is getting dark, and we are running out of time.

I blink back my tears, "Listen, we've got to get that mirror back. Put your hand down in there and try to grab it."

But his hand won't fit. I try mine. I can get it mostly in, but it just isn't long enough to reach the floor.

Thomas speaks up, "Okay, I've got a plan. My brother Tim has a skinny arm, and it should be long enough. But the streetlights are coming on and we are out of time."

"Thom-as!" I try not to cry.

"Timmy will help us. First thing tomorrow let's meet here and I'll get him to come."

"Thomas, your brothers never help us. They always tease us. How will you get him to come?"

"Trust me, he'll come. I found some dirty magazines under his bed. If he doesn't help us, I'll tell my dad and he'll get in so much trouble."

"Wow, you're brave. Okay, first thing tomorrow!"

We head in opposite directions as both of our moms holler our names from our back porches.

I get home and go straight to my room. I sit down at my vanity and pick up the hairbrush that matches my mirror, "Don't worry little Karen Brush. We'll rescue little Karen Mirror in the morning. She'll be okay."

I don't sleep well that night and as soon as I finish my strawberry Pop-Tart and orange Hi-C breakfast, I call Thomas on the phone in the kitchen.

"Thomas, I couldn't sleep. My poor special mirror is all alone in that house. Did you get Timmy to help us? Are you ready to meet?"

"Karen, we've got a problem. Meet me out on the sidewalk."

I run out to the front sidewalk. He wasn't kidding. We have a major problem. There is a moving truck in the Franco's driveway. The new family is moving in. I grab Thomas' hand, and we run straight to my backyard where we sit down in lawn chairs, face-to-face.

"Thomas O'Neill, I'm a goner. Those new people have opened the front door and saw my little Karen mirror and her back of head looks just like my back of head and they are going to know I tried to break in and I am going to jail!"

Thomas stands up and starts running down my driveway back towards his house.

"You're right! I'll visit you in jail! Bye!"

I jump up.

"THOMAS MATTHEW O'NEILL YOU GET BACK HERE THIS INSTANT! FOR BETTER OR WORSE! FOR BETTER OR WORSE! GET BACK HERE!!!"

He never even slows down. I climb the back stairs to my house and make my way slowly up to my room, waiting for the sirens that will bring the police to take me to jail.

MOXIE MATTERS

Bowling League

In wintertime, my brother Dave and three of his friends decide to have a bowling team. The moms of these boys have daughters too and they sign us up at the bowling alley to play in a littler girls league at the same time. We don't even get a choice! But I don't even care because the bowling league is so fun. Dave's team is Dave, Craig, Skip, and Rick. Our team is L'il Dave, L'il Craig, L'il Skip, and L'il Rick. Rick didn't have a little sister but a friend of one of the other girls slides into that spot and we still called her L'il Rick.

Grandpa Modder bowls pretty much every day of his life, so Dad said bowling is in our DNA. We all smush into someone's car and drive to the bowling alley. Walking inside, our eyes adjust to the smoky darkness. An adult league is always ending and when I walk up to the lanes sometimes their ashtrays will still be smoldering. I love it—it smells just like home.

None of us are serious enough to have our own balls, bags, and shoes, so we have to go to the counter and get a pair of shoes. We give them our own shoes to make sure we return the nasty bowling shoes. As if we'd even ever keep them. Ick! Then we hurry to pick out a ball. I am the youngest and really need the lightest ball out there. But the bigger girls in our league don't care who is the smallest and sometimes I have to play with a ten-pound ball! That isn't fair.

We all play our games and then have a quick snack before getting picked up. I am glad Dad always sends us with some money for pop and candy or whatever. On the ride home from

55

bowling league, the eight of us will smush into another parent's car. My favorite ride home is when the dad is blasting, We Are the Champions on the radio and we all hang out the car windows scream-singing at the top of our lungs.

The End Of Scouts For This Girl

I've been a Brownie Girl Scout all year and don't like it one bit. We meet on Wednesdays, after school. Wednesdays! When we get out of school thirty minutes early for a weekly teacher meeting. Thirty extra minutes to play with my friends or plan a new show. But no, I've had to go to Brownies every stinking Wednesday.

Well, Brownies is finally over and today is the bridging ceremony in the auditorium. At least I won't have to wear the dumb brown beanie hat and uniform anymore. Green is more my color anyway.

Mrs. Crabbyface (not her actual name but it suits her) calls me to the stage (the STAGE!) to cross the proverbial Brownie bridge to become a full-fledged Girl Scout…and she says my name wrong. The horror! Holding a blessed microphone, I anticipate hearing Karen Modder, being crooned as each name is called alphabetically.

"Kirsten Mahler… Karen M-oh-der…"

What? What did she just say? Karen M-oh-der? No! This kind of mistake is what led to my mean nickname: Motor Mouth. The heat rises on my cheeks and my ears feel so hot that I think flames are bursting right out of the tops of them. I march right up to Mrs. Crabbyface, pull the microphone from her hairy hands and in a loud and proud voice I say, "M-ah-der. It's Modder, Karen MODDER."

I hand the microphone back to her, bow to the parents in the audience, and continue across the stage. Later that afternoon, my parents are told that I am not "scout material" and can't return to the troop for fourth grade. That uniform is itchy anyway. I'll just put it in with my other costumes moving forward.

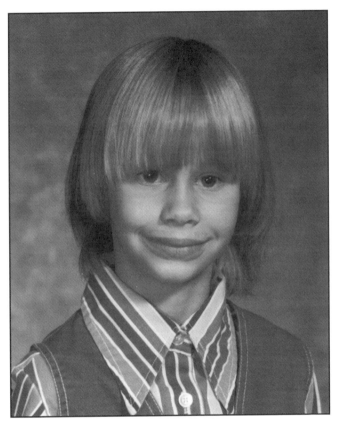

Kick The Can, Summer 1979

The air is thick with summertime humidity and anticipation as the sun is starting to set. Thomas, Mary, Katherine, and I sit on my driveway and watch as our older brothers and sisters gather in the street. Will it be a night of Kick the Can or Ghost in the Graveyard?

An even bigger question on my mind is whether these big kids are going to allow us little kids to join the chosen game. Thomas and I steal a hopeful glance at each other. It's up to our older brothers whether we will get in. More kids walk up from around the corner and a few even come from down the hill. If they get enough, they won't need us. We hold our breath, and we wait. Mary and Katherine hate night games and just want to watch TV. They stand up and head inside Katherine's house. Not Thomas and me. We've waited a long time and can't believe our luck when Timmy looks our way and gives us the nod.

We're in!

Kick the Can is chosen, and I offer to run into our house to grab the near-empty Folgers coffee can. You can bet that if we get to play, I'm going to become the best, most helpful kick-the-canner on the block. I run into the house, zip to the kitchen cabinet, and grab the Folgers. I dump the remaining coffee straight into the garbage as my mom pulls her Benson & Hedges cigarette out of her mouth in protest.

"Hey! That wasn't empty!"

As I run out the back door, I yell, "Sorry Mom! But I'm IN! Thomas and I finally get to play!"

In a flash, I am back with the group and the can is placed in the center of the street. The rules on every street in the neighborhood are different. Ours on Lenox Street are simple: One person is "it" and everyone else goes to hide somewhere between the corner and

O'Neill's house, front yards only, while the "it" player sits on the nearby curb, covers their eyes, and counts to 100. At 100, "it" begins the hunt and starts to search out hiding players. If they see you, they must call out your name and where you are hiding.

That's when it gets exciting! If you're hiding and "it" calls you out, it's a race to the can! Whomever gets there first kicks the can. If "it" kicks it, the other person is in jail and must sit on the curb in the jail spot. If the hiding person kicks the can, everyone in jail is free, and "it" must count all over again while everyone hides. The game ends when "it" finds everyone, and everyone is in jail.

No one wants us little kids to be "it" first because we hadn't yet proven ourselves to be worthy. As soon as the first "it" hits the curb to count, we all take off. Of course, I go straight to my favorite spot, behind the evergreens on our front lawn. I like this spot because it's close to the can and I for sure want to be able to outrun "it" and kick that precious coffee can if I am found.

I lay flat on my stomach in the dirt, over on the side of the hedge so I can have eyes on "it." They begin to capture one kid after another. I'm getting bored after waiting forever. I didn't know my hiding spot was that good. I want to rescue everyone and I'm feeling bold. The jail is really crowded, and I make my move.

While "it" is facing away from me, I stand up and start to walk slowly toward the can. A stupid friend of "it" alerts them to my move and they yell, "I see Karen, on her lawn!" We both take off. I might be considered a little kid, but I am so fast. I make it to the can first, give it a giant kick, and free all the jailed kids!

Triumph!

Glory!

Not only did I free the big kids, but I secure our spot in night games forever. It feels so good to be growing up!

MOXIE MATTERS

TV

TV time means time together as a family, or at least part of the family. We have two color television sets in our home. The larger TV is the focus of the family room at the back of the house. The long antennae at the top of the box guarantee us channels 2, 5, 7, 9, 11, 32, and 44. My brother is the only one who watches a program on 44—Speed Racer, and I rarely watch with him.

I love everything about TV. I easily get lost in the stories of Charlie's Angels, Jonathan and Jennifer Hart, the crew of The Love Boat, the often scary stories played out on Fantasy Island. I want more than anything to be a guest on any of the variety shows. I know that Sonny and Cher, the Osmonds, or even Carol Burnett would be great teachers if I could somehow get on their shows. When Saturday Night Live debuted in 1975, my older siblings wouldn't let me stay up with them and watch. As soon as I am old enough, I will be glued to the set for the full ninety minutes.

My favorite nights are when I get to watch my favorite shows alone. Luckily, that happens a lot as my parents go out most Friday and Saturday nights. If they are home, Mom can be found sitting up in her bed, watching their smaller set perched on her dresser. I think my mom may love watching TV more than I do.

At almost any time of day, I can walk into my parents' bedroom and find Mom either sitting up, two pillows behind her back, legs outstretched and crossed at the ankles, or lying on her right side with one pillow folded in half under her head. She is always transfixed with whatever is on the screen.

"Mom? Can I come in? What are you watching?"

I ask quietly just in case she is taking a nap. She likes to take a lot of naps.

"Yes, come in, I'm awake!"

I enter her room. Not only is she awake, but she has some of her favorite things around her. In her hand is a lit Benson & Hedges cigarette, green glass ashtray on the nightstand nearby. On a coaster next to the ashtray is a cold can of Tab and in her lap is a bowl of bright red pistachio nuts. She works the nuts open with her long fingernails when she puts the cigarette into her mouth.

I climb into the bed beside her and together we watch an old black and white film. I don't care that the movie has already started when I arrive, I am so happy to enter Mom's realm: the kingdom that is her bedroom. I don't mind the smoke, or the crack of the shells. I don't even really mind that she doesn't share.

If Mom isn't in her room, watching TV, or taking one of her many naps, she can be found in either the basement doing laundry, sitting at the built-in desk area of our kitchen table on the phone with her friends, or, and this last one is only ever at night, pacing back and forth in the living room in total darkness, lit cigarette in action, record on the stereo.

4th Grade

In 4th grade, I stay in PROBE and thankfully my teacher, Miss Clawman, likes Probe and there are more kids in my grade who are in it now so that is even better. Miss Clawman thinks I am funny, and it is easy to be on her good side. She even lives in our neighborhood. She can walk to school!

One day, my friends and I get a bold idea and present it to Miss Clawman. Let me back things up a bit. Miss Clawman has a nickname, "The Claw." I honestly don't know why. She is tall, very thin, and a tiny bit stooped at the shoulders. She has strawberry blond hair and glasses and kids think she is mean. Parents talk about her being a spinster because "she is still single at her age." Thomas, Jim, Stacy, and I think she is nice. One day we ask her if we could come to her house for dinner. And can you believe it? She says yes!

Our foursome is nervous and excited, and our parents can't even believe we have the nerve to ask. Thomas and I walk down the block to Stacy's and then we walk to Miss Clawman's house. Jim lives close to her and meets us on the sidewalk out front. Thomas gathers us together before we walk up to the front door and hands us each a pair of white gloves.

"You guys, I brought these because I think it will be so hysterical if we put them on before we go in. We tell her it's for a "white glove test." Then we walk around and see if she's got any dust on her furniture by running our finger over things."

We put on the gloves. We ring the doorbell. Miss Clawman opens the door and invites us onto her porch. Thomas holds up his hands and gives us all a look. We hold up our gloved hands as well.

"Miss Clawman, we are honored to be at your home. Before we eat, it's our duty to inspect all areas of your home for dust."

"Welcome children. You may inspect each room on the first floor of my home, but that is all. You may enter."

And we do. We walk in and proceed to run our white-gloved fingers over every surface of her living room and dining room. Not a single speck of dust is to be found! She passes the white glove test with flying colors, and we all giggle—even Miss Clawman. She feeds us a mystery casserole with large glasses of milk and pudding for dessert. Chocolate pudding!

Miss Clawman is quickly going to the top of my favorite teacher list. After our goodbyes, we all walk home, absolutely satisfied that Miss Clawman is no one to be feared. In fact, she is a very kind woman and we make it our mission to let the community know her nickname, "The Claw," is way off track and shouldn't be used anymore.

For some reason, we hold great influence over our classmates and her reputation is changed quickly after our self-invited dinner with the white glove test. The four of us kids have a reputation of our own. We are mostly known as being nice and being funny. We include kids.

At recess, everyone is invited to play kickball, tag, or have races on the 50-yard track painted on the back part of the playground. Birthday parties happen after school, on your given birthday, and almost always involve inviting either your entire class, or just the boys/girls. Everyone brings their presents to school and the whole crew walks home with the birthday kid and eats cake, drinks fruit punch (pop if it is a fancy party), and plays games like pin the tail on the donkey or musical chairs. You open presents and then parents show up for pick up. Life is simple and life is fun!

Friends

I close my worn-out copy of one of the many Encyclopedia Brown books in my collection and sit up on my bed. Should I read another book or go find my friends? With a quick glance out of my green metallic blinds, I see the sun is shining. Perfect day for some crime-fighting!

At the top of the stairs, I have a big decision to make. Dare I jump them all straight to the landing? Should I slide down the thick banister and hope I don't slide off the other side to certain death? After only a moment's thought, I opt to slide down on my stomach, hands first. I'll be a crazy crocodile hunting for food. At the landing I switch it up and tuck my pretend walkie-talkie into the back of my shorts as I yell, "Mom! Dad! I'm going outside to play!"

"Okay, come back when the streetlights come on!"

I casually walk out the back door, scheming up our mission should my friends choose to accept it. Once I hit the bottom step, I decide to start at Thomas's house. I skip to the bottom of our driveway and when I hit the sidewalk, I decide on a full sprint past the four houses that separate us. I slow myself down as I reach their back door and take the steps two at a time before knocking.

"Hi Mr. O'Neill! Can Thomas play?"

Mr. O'Neill rubs the sleep out of his eyes as he scratches his stomach with both hands.

"Hold on. Thomas? You've got a friend here!"

Thomas pads to the door, his sweat socks flopping as he walks. As the youngest of four boys, his clothes are all hand-me-downs. The fact that he's shorter than the average kid doesn't help, and he always seems to be swimming in whatever he wears. I can barely contain my joy that he's home. Now I've just got to make sure he wants to play.

"Hi Thomas! Do you want to play?"

"Yeah, sure! Let me get my shoes on." A moment later he yells to his folks, "I'm going out to play with Karen!"

"Okay, be back when the streetlights come on!"

Excellent!

"Okay, Thomas, here's what I'm thinking: Charlie's Angels. We check if Mary and Katherine are home and if they are, we're set. If they aren't, then Hart to Hart. Let's get Katherine first because if she can't play then Mary can be Max the butler for Hart to Hart. What do you think?"

"Yeah, yeah, okay! Smart! Let's start with Katherine."

We get to the end of his driveway and carefully look left, then right. No cars! We run across the street and turn right. Two houses later we are at the Jablonskis. Katherine is a year younger than us and goes to the Catholic school. She is tiny and thin, and I am always afraid she is going to break. Her brown glasses always need a push to stay up on her nose and magnify her eyes just enough to make her look smart. She always wants to play with us and pretty much takes any role we assign her in our games.

"Thomas, you knock. Her dad scares me a little."

"He scares me too, you knock!"

"Ugh, fine."

Knock, knock, knock. No answer.

"Ring the bell."

"You ring the bell!"

"Okay fine, I'll ring it."

Ding dong.

We hear footsteps coming to the door and then it opens just a crack. It's the elusive Mr. Jablonski, the angry junk man who we don't see too often because he is always out driving his truck around "looking for more junk to sell at those God-awful flea markets" as the adults in the neighborhood say.

"Um, hi Mr. Jablonski, can Katherine play?"

"I've told you kids not to ring the bell!"

"Yes, yes you did. We knocked but no one answered, and we are really hoping Katherine can play."

"Hold on."

He shuts the door, and we just look at each other, unsure of what's coming next. A few moments later, tiny Katherine is sliding out the door.

"I can play for a little bit, until my dad calls me."

"Great! Here's what we're thinking, Mary's house next, and if she can play…Charlie's Angels!"

"Again? Oh, okay, that sounds fun."

Together, we set off down her driveway and take a left turn at the sidewalk. I think we should hop on one foot the three houses to Mary's, and everyone agrees. We catch our breath in front of Mary's back door, and I knock.

"Hi Theresa, is Mary home?"

Mary's big sister Theresa is so cool. She's wearing an awesome poncho, and her hair is so pretty. It's darker than any hair I've ever seen and is straight as a board and shiny as the sun. She's kind of mean though.

Theresa growls, "Ugh. I thought you were my friends. Mary! Mary! Your little friends are here!"

Mary makes it to the door with a big smile.

"Hi guys, what's up?"

"Do you want to play Charlie's Angels with us?"

This is a risky question as Mary is two whole years older than Thomas and I, three years older than Katherine. We never know when she's going to hit the point where she doesn't want to play with us anymore.

We hold our breath.

"Yes! Let me get my shoes and I'll be right out."

Mary's hair isn't as dark as her big sister's. It's kind of a chocolate-y brown and instead of shiny, it's kind of frizzy. She tries to control her locks with a blow-dryer, but it doesn't work, and she cries about it sometimes. I think her big waves are cool!

We park ourselves on my favorite part of Mary's backyard… her canopied bench swing. Only three of us fit, but Mary is happy to stand and face us. As we swing, I lay out my plan.

"If it's okay with you guys, we could each pick the Angel we want to be. Thomas, are you okay to be Bosley?"

"Yes, who else would I be?"

"Exactly. Okay, I'd like to be Chris Munroe."

Katherine quietly responds, "My hair is blonder than yours and it's feathered just like Chris', so I think I should be Chris."

Mary agrees.

"Yeah, Katherine should be Chris."

"But she's always Chris! I really want a turn being Chris."

Mary says, "I'm oldest so I decide. Katherine is Chris and I want to be Kelly Garrett."

"But you're always Kelly! It's not fair. I want to be someone besides Sabrina Duncan!"

Thomas speaks up, "Listen Karen. Katherine looks the most like Chris and Mary and Kelly both have brown hair. You make a really good Sabrina! Be Sabrina."

Everyone stares at me. What choice do I have? Every single time we play, I try to be Chris. Every single time we play I end up being Sabrina. Well, at least she is the "smart one." Once it is decided, Thomas/Bosley takes the lead and gathers us Angels around the backyard table for our assignment from Charlie.

This time, there is a kidnapping and we work together, traveling around the block, to solve the mystery and rescue the imaginary victim. Just as we wrap things up, we hear Katherine's dad calling for her. Her parents are the strictest, so she runs straight home. I turn to my remaining friends.

"What do you think? Switch to Hart to Hart? I can be Jennifer, Thomas is Jonathan, and Mary, you can be Max our butler?"

Thomas looks at his watch. Then he looks down the block and sees his big brothers playing frisbee.

"Nah, I'm done for today. I'm going home."

He leaves and I know he is worried that his brothers think he is dumb for playing with girls. I think that's pretty dumb. Good thing there is still lots of time before the streetlights come on.

"Mary, what do you think? Should we scavenge for more items for the club house?"

"Okay, if you want to!"

There is a little nook on the back side of Mary's house that is sheltered by bushes and a fence on the street side, her house on one, and the Motts' house on the other. Her parents don't care if we hang out there and we like to look around the neighborhood for treasures to add to it.

We know we can only really search in a two-block radius, and we take off after enjoying our favorite snack from Mary's kitchen. Her family introduced me to the two most incredible edible creations I'd ever known—OJ 7's and Wheat Thin crackers. OJ 7's are a simple delight that make my taste buds sing. Are you ready for it? You mix equal parts orange juice with 7-Up. That's it! Refreshing, fun, and looks like one of the cocktails our parents enjoy. And Wheat Thins—a perfect square of salty goodness. Man, I love the snacks at Mary's house.

Mary and I decide to take our drinks and crackers on our walk as we set out to find anything great for our fort. About half a block into our foray, we find an actual couch out on the curb! What a find! It will go perfectly right up again the fence.

"Let's go get my wagon and we can load this up and bring it to your yard. It's perfect! We can just put a blanket or something over that stain."

"Oh Karen, I don't know what my parents will think."

"Mary, it's fantastic! Look at that pattern."

I point to the brown floral print that drew my eye when I first saw this gem down the block.

"Trust me Mary. It will be in the backyard, around the corner. They may never even see it! Or, when they see it, they will LOVE it. It's perfect. We can have meetings there and plan things."

"What kind of meetings? What are we planning?"

"Geez, I don't know! We can start a club, we can plan some shows, we can have Charlie give us our assignments…look how comfortable it looks. Come on, let's get my wagon."

I easily talk Mary into grabbing the couch and hauling it to her back yard. Her parents never even see us navigating the thing down the street, up her driveway, and to the back corner fort zone. We struggle to get it off the wagon, but we make it! What a find. Mary goes back in the house to grab more Wheat Thins and I put my feet up as I plan all of the plans we would plan on our new find.

As soon as it starts getting dark, we run to the front of her house. As the streetlights start to flicker on, I decide to skip home in honor of the wonderful day we've had.

The very next morning, I wake up and open my window blinds on a new day wondering what adventures await me. I gaze across the street at Mary's house and can't believe it. Our couch is on her front curb! I put on my favorite pink satin shorts and a t-shirt. Today I grab a pair of knee socks because I decide to skate over to Mary's to find out what happened.

"Mom, I'm going to Mary's quick! Be right back!"

"Okay, come home when the streetlights come on!"

"Mom! It's morning! I'll be right back!"

I sit on the bottom step of the stairs on our back porch and lace up my pride and joy, my blue-with-white-striped gym-shoe roller skates. Quick as a wink, I am down the driveway, across the street, and up Mary's driveway knocking on her back door.

A crabby-faced Mr. Bandino opens the door. But I am not fooled. He looks crabby, but he is super nice and I can always make him laugh.

"Hi Mr. Bandino! Is Ka…"

"Karen Modder, I was told you brought that hideous couch and put it in my backyard yesterday. Is that true?"

"Yes, isn't it wonderful? We got it for our fort that Mrs. Bandino said we could have back there. Don't you love it?"

"No. No, I do not and that's why it's at the curb where it belongs. No fort. No furniture. No playing with Mary today. Good-bye."

"Oh, sorry Mr. Bandino. Good-bye. Tell Mary hi and I'm sorry! I sure love those Wheat Thins you always let me eat. Give the missus a big hug from me."

He shuts the door just as a smile is creeping onto his face—I just knew it! I skate down the driveway and sit on the glorious couch one last time.

Fun In An Unfinished Basement

Go down the basement stairs, five steps, landing full of dirty laundry. Turn right, down six more steps to the basement. These last steps you can see through when you are going back up.

To the left, built-in shelf/cabinets against the wall. Then beyond that on the left, our ping pong table. On the right, our air hockey table with the game table resting on top. The front of the house at the far end with the old green couches from the family room set up in an L for seating.

My focus now is on the ping pong table, or rather under the ping pong table.

Thomas and I love to play Hart to Hart. He pretends to be Jonathan and I pretend to be Jennifer Hart. We are a fabulously wealthy couple who solve mysteries and fight crime. Our trusty butler Max is often part of our adventures. Mary always volunteers to be Max. One of Max's biggest jobs is as chauffeur of Jonathan and Jennifer's limousine.

Well, that's how we play it anyway.

My sister got a super cool gym mat for her birthday or Christmas or something and she never actually uses it, so I decide it is mine. I honestly don't think she even knows I commandeered that thing, but I spend hours using it. As a base layer for our limo, and then for years perfecting my front and back walkovers, limbers, and round-offs for hours at a time at night when I think I might become a professional gymnast.

This mat isn't what you think of when you think of a gym mat. It is a putty color and doesn't fold up like the school gym mats. The only way to make it smaller is to roll it up and it takes up a good bit of space. Rolling it up provides whole new imaginative uses for it!

But for now, Thomas, Mary, and I roll it up and slide it over to the top of the ping pong table. Then we unroll it down the length of the table. It is a perfect fit! And so comfortable for all of our upcoming travels. We then take the pillows from the couches. The bench-like layout of the couch mimics perfect limo seats! The base, seat-part is simple but propping up the back is tricky. We end up grabbing books from the nearby cabinets to stack behind the "back" part of the seats, successfully propping them up.

Our limo is taking shape! What we need next are the fun things that make a limo special—snack and drinks! While Mary and Thomas make the front section ready for Max, our butler/driver, I go up to the kitchen to scope out some supplies. I grab some bottles of Pepsi (that we will pretend is booze) and a bag of Doritos. I love Doritos and thankfully, Mom keeps a good supply of them on top of the fridge.

Thomas is rifling through our old toy box, the one with sliding chalkboard doors angled on the front with two narrow shelves above. I love that toy box! You can hide toys while displaying your favorites. He finds my old toy phone and a few other gadgets to add to the vehicle that is shaping up quite nicely.

Once the limo is ready, our imaginations take over and we fall into character.

"Jonathan, darling, whatever shall we do tonight?"

"Oh, I don't know dear, why don't we go to our favorite restaurant, Chez Paul?"

"Yes, darling, that would be fabulous. Max!"

"Mrs. H?"

"Max darling, please get the car ready. We are going to Chez Paul."

"Yes, Mrs. Hart."

"And Max…"

"Yes?"

"Be a dear and make sure we've got some snacks for the ride."

"All set Mrs. H!"

Thomas and I enter our limo and set off for Chez Paul. But of course, the phone will ring on our way, sending us off to solve a murder mystery, or to catch a diamond thief. Mary will work closely with us as we often leave my basement and travel around my house and even outside following imaginary clues. We always, always solve our mysteries before the streetlights come on and they have to go back home.

On rare occasions, Dad will interrupt our crime-solving to offer us the actual keys to his actual car! He tells us we can't actually drive anywhere—darn it!—but we can pretend to drive! If Mary/Max is playing with us, she'll sit in the front seat and we climb into the back. Mary is a couple of years older so we can't always convince her to play with us, especially when we are outside, in the front yard, in the car, in the driveway. I think her older brothers and sisters tease her for playing. But when she isn't with us, we just "drive" ourselves.

Thomas is such a great friend. Our imaginations are often in sync and our adventures will sometimes even last into the nighttime. This only ever happens on weekends or in the summertime. Our parents are good friends, and they often spend time together drinking fancy drinks called martinis, manhattans, and Tia Maria. If our parents are laughing together, we play and play right until bedtime. It is usually at our house because Thomas has three older brothers. They definitely tease him for always hanging out with me and call me his girlfriend. They are dopes though because we got married the summer before kindergarten.

Dinnertime

Monday night, 6:15, dinnertime at the Modder house.

"Susan, it's Monday, your night to start the prayer."

"Okay! Lord, bless this food for Jesus' sake. Amen."

"David."

"Ugh. Lord bless this food for Jesus' sake amen."

"Very nice. Karen?"

"LordblessthisfoodforJesus'sakeamen."

"Karen, this is not a race. Try again."

I giggle.

"Lord! Bless this FOOD for Jesus' SAKE!! Amen!"

We dig in.

The Modder family has assigned seats at the dinner table and a who-starts-the-prayer rotation that is solid. Susan starts the prayer on Mondays and Thursdays, then we take turns by age—David then me. David starts the prayer on Tuesdays and Fridays, then me and Susan. I get to lead on Wednesdays and Saturdays, then Susan and David. If we ever forget, it is also what is called counter-clockwise around the table.

Our kitchen table is mostly round. I sit on the end that connects the table to the wall by the TV room. Mom is next to me on the left, David in the middle, then Dad, and Susan on the other end by Mom's desk/where the phone is. We always have to sit in our assigned spot. I don't think it's fair. Susan gets to answer the phone if it rings during dinnertime. Well, only if Mom or Dad are expecting a call because otherwise it is rude to call people during dinnertime so we will not answer.

We also always have to say the same exact prayer. My dad and his brother and sister grew up saying the same prayer but in Dutch. It sounds like this, "Hege sege dayza spiza. Amen." We don't know if this is the right way in Dutch so we say it in English. I always try to say it super fast, with a silly voice, or really any way I can jazz it up. Mom and Dad pretty much get angry every time I do this. But I do it anyway. I think God probably likes it when I make it sound more interesting.

Sundays are my favorite dinner night. Us kids are allowed to eat in the TV room on snack trays! We are only allowed to eat in there on Sundays for dinner, when we are sick, or when my parents are having a party and then we get frozen Swanson's TV dinners and get to eat in there to stay out of everyone's way (which, on the one hand, is exciting, and on the other hand, I dislike because I love to help with the parties).

Back to dinner! On Sundays, The Wonderful World of Disney will come on channel 7 at 6:00. We set up our snack trays just before, load up our dinner plates, and sit on the couches to eat our meals. The best part is that it is just us three kids! Mom and Dad stay in the kitchen! We are always excited because the show is good and without parents watching us, we swap out all our food with each other. I don't like vegetables, but Susan does so she eats mine. Then I'll eat whatever she doesn't want. If it's not vegetables or liver, I'll eat it!

Let me stop right here and tell you about the one and only time I ate liver. 6:15 and we all sit at the dinner table. Mom says what we are having is like Minute Steak with grilled onions on the top. It's one of her favorites and I'm excited because I love steak. Mom has a big smile and I'm so happy she's made something new and…it's like steak! The color is weird, but I cut off a piece and take a big bite. I try to swallow it but the taste is so bad. The taste is so bad that I cannot help myself and throw up on the kitchen table. Dad is yelling at me. David is laughing. Susan runs from the table holding her hand over her mouth. Mom sends me to my room.

Later she tells me that steak was called liver and I ask her if liver is really steak. She tells me to watch my smart mouth. But why is it smart? I really wanted to know. She never made liver again. I think my barfing kind of ruined it for everyone.

You want to know what else makes me feel like barfing? All vegetables. No, I take it back. I like lettuce, tomatoes, and corn on the cob. All other vegetables are disgusting. Every single night that Mom makes dinner, she makes vegetables to go with them. Every single night I am not allowed to leave the dinner table until I eat every last bite of vegetables. Except glorious Sunday nights when I can get my brother and sister to eat them for me.

I have tricks up my sleeve when it comes to eating vegetables. Let's start with peas. For a while, peas were my favorite because I could easily take them carefully off my plate, one at a time, slide them under the dinner plate and smush the plate back down flat. Or, peas could hide under a pork chop or a chicken bone. If I did the plate smash, I'd just offer to clean up the dinner dishes that night so Mom could have a break. Except one night when I forgot and left the table to go play with friends. No more plate smushing for me. But peas were still good because the peas are about the same size as my allergy pill and I swallow those suckers four times a day. So now if peas are on the plate, I swallow them whole, one at a time.

Swallowing whole vegetables works for most any vegetable Mom pops out of a can and into the microwave to get heated. I can say I've swallowed every vegetable in one swallow—even nasty Brussel sprouts. I only did one sprout that way because I nearly choked, and it hurt my throat so bad that my neck was sore for a day. I cut those guys into four pieces now and swallow each one. I drink almost a whole gallon of milk a night swallowing everything.

Mom is fed up with my "dinnertime antics." She argues with me almost every night to eat my vegetables "normally."

"Mom, God didn't make me to like vegetables, so I am doing my best. If you do not like how I eat these things, then please do not put any on my plate."

"Watch your smart mouth."

"You watch my smart mouth while it swallows this green bean."

I don't get sent to my room because I can't leave the table until all my vegetables are gone.

If it's a really bad one, like beets, I just don't eat it. Mom does not like it when I make this choice. Dad doesn't seem to care if I eat my stupid vegetables, but he says I have to do what Mom says. He usually leaves the table.

I have two ideas for how to handle the worst of the worst: broccoli, beets, cauliflower, Brussel sprouts…pretty much anything but the peas I can easily swallow in one gulp:

1. Excuse myself to go to the bathroom. I am sure that if I sit on the toilet long enough, Mom will give up and clear the table. This will let me go on with my evening of prime time TV watching. The good shows start at 7:00 so I have to plan things very carefully. I will eat every other bite of food on my plate, and then say, "Mom, my stomach hurts. I think I have to go big potty, and it might be the runs." [side note: In our family, we were not allowed to say poop, pee, fart, and diarrhea was questionable. The substitutions were big potty, tinkle, foo-foo, and the runs.]

I will go to the bathroom, take a seat on the toilet, and start the waiting game. When I feel a very long time has passed, I will come out and carefully walk back to the kitchen table, leaning forward to see if my plate has been cleared. It is never, ever, never, ever cleared. Mom is always waiting, usually with her feet up and a lit cigarette between her fingers, a fresh cup of coffee in front of her. Then I eat the now cold, even nastier culprits on my plate.

2. Play the waiting game with silent treatment. I say something like, "Mother, eating this food on my plate will kill me. I cannot do it. You cannot make me." I will then lean back, tilt my head, and cross my arms over my chest. At this point, the rest of the family is usually clearing their plates and heading to the TV room. Mom starts a fresh pot of coffee, grabs a clean ashtray, puts her feet up on

the chair next to her, and crosses her arms over her chest. I wait. She waits. The clock ticks on. The 7:00 shows start. I tilt my head to the left. She lights another Benson & Hedges. The 7:30 shows start. One hour until bedtime. I don't want to miss the shows but this is not right. I should not have to eat something that may kill me. I tilt my head to the right. She pours another cup of coffee. I look straight ahead and my mind starts racing. Now the beans are slimy. Oh gosh. They look even worse than before. No way will she make me eat them. I peek over at her. She looks comfortable. I know I'm in trouble. But darn it, I will not eat these.

It's almost my bedtime and of course, I'll have to leave the table to go to bed. 8:30 comes and goes. Now I'm scared. I refuse to speak. She looks like she's enjoying the quiet time. I don't think this is working. Oh no! I hold out until 9:15 and then I pinch my nose with my thumb and pointer finger while I shove the horrible beans in my mouth, chewing as fast as I can with my mouth open and then washing the mess down with my warm milk. I take my dishes to the sink with tears in my eyes. Mom stands up and gives me a hug. "Vegetables are important and they will help you grow and be strong. You will always eat your vegetables."

I never once, not once left the table without eating my vegetables. But I really tried.

Turning 10

Turning ten is a big deal in my family. On March 17, 1980, I will be ten years old. Three major things will happen. I know this because I am the youngest kid and I get whatever my brother and sister got when they turned ten.

First, at ten years old, I will get a house key! This means that I will be able to come and go as I please from the front door of the house. It means that I am old enough to be alone in the house and if I leave, I will lock it with the front door key. This is important stuff. Also, because I am the youngest kid, I never get to be alone. I cannot wait to be alone and watch what I want on TV, talk on the phone, or just blast music from my radio. I'm almost an adult at ten years old.

Second, at ten years old, I will get a ten-speed bike for my birthday. I CANNOT WAIT FOR THIS TO HAPPEN. I am hoping for a green Schwinn. Sue and David have blue ones and I want my favorite color and that is green. Dear God, if you love me, even a little bit, please let my parents know how important a green Schwinn is to me. Thank you and amen.

And finally, at ten years old, I will be allowed to finally babysit for money! Sue is almost sixteen and she's ready to hand over her clients to me. I love little kids and I love having money so this should work out really good. I'll have a 10-speed, hopefully green, and so I will be able to get myself to, and from, jobs.

My whole world will be so much better when I am ten years old. I will get jobs, have spending money, and my own wheels (powered by gears!) to get anywhere I need to go. It is going to be more wonderful than anything I've ever dreamed of!

Ten years old...here I come!

My babysitting gigs start off easy enough. I've been a mother's helper for Mrs. Kelly, two houses down for a while now. Natalie is so cute and fun to play with! The Kelly's still think I am a little young to be alone with Natalie but now they pay me $1 for every hour that I come over and play with her. Sounds like a good deal to me!

The Ladies' Lounge

"Karen, go find your mother."

Church is over and it's time to go home. Dad is rounding up everyone in the family and we don't see Mom in the fellowship hall. I go to the big room next door with all of the couches and chairs. I walk around and don't see her anywhere. Well, there's only one place left…The Ladies' Lounge.

If you want to smoke a cigarette at our church, then you've got to go down to the basement, to The Ladies' Lounge. I'm excited she's down there for two reasons. I love the basement of our church, and if Mom is having a smoke in The Ladies' Lounge, she's probably with her friends and they are so much fun!

Let e describe the basement. Off the main, first floor hallway, there is a long, wide staircase that heads to the basement. But it's not a scary basement! The first room in the basement is the nursery for all of the babies and toddlers. The nursery is huge with all kinds of toys. My favorite, even as a big kid, is the teeter-totter-like thing that sits two or three little kids on each side, next to each other like a bench. They lean forward and hold onto a bar, and they face their friends on the other side. Then you rock and giggle and it's so much fun! One medium-sized big kid can sit on either side and rock, and I've seen teenagers stand on it with one foot on either bench! It's painted white and it is my favorite thing in that fun room.

The room right next door to the nursery is the Luther League Room. Luther League is the very clever name of the high school youth group. This room is quiet, the walls are lined with shelves that hold books like the Bible, study books, and games. There are tables and chairs and couches too. It looks so cool in there but I never go in. Teenagers are a little scary to me so I just peek in the windows on the door and keep it moving.

Past the Luther League room is The Ladies' Lounge. There isn't a door on the lounge, but a big, walk-through entry. The lounge has a couch, chairs, coffee table, and side tables. All of the tables hold ashtrays because The Ladies' Lounge is the only place the women of the church can go and have a smoke. My mom and her friends seem like the bosses of The Ladies' Lounge to me. I am pretty sure my dad, and the other husbands, are afraid of what happens in there. I'm also pretty sure that those women are solving the church problems, their family problems, and the problems of the whole world while they puff away. Whenever I walk up, they stop talking right away. I think they quiet down because they are excited to see me and want to hear what I have to say.

Then beyond the lounge room is the toilet room. Let me tell you the cutest thing about the toilet room. The first stall has a teeny, tiny toilet for the littlest kid butts—just like kindergarten. It is the cutest thing I have ever seen. When I was a really little kid, I loved that toilet because the hole on the seat was extra small so you couldn't fall in. It is my favorite toilet anywhere. And I've seen a lot of toilets.

After a quick look into the Luther League room, I skip into the lounge and find my mom, legs crossed, cigarette in hand, smoke cloud circling, laughing with Mrs. Nielsen, Mrs.

Olsen, and Mrs. Zimmermann is there today too!

"Hi everyone!"

Silence.

"Mom, Dad said it's time to go. You ladies should probably all go to, church is emptying out upstairs."

"Tell Dad I'll be up when I finish this cigarette."

"It's okay, I'll just wait."

I wedge myself in next to mom. She probably wants to snuggle because she hasn't seen me in about an hour. She puts her arm around me and I tell the ladies not to mind me, they can keep talking.

Mrs. Zimmermann laughs.

"Karen, you are something else!"

"Thank you!"

I beam. This is a great compliment!

The ladies chat about some more things but I don't even listen. I love my mom's friends. They laugh a LOT and are always nice to me. My mom likes to drive over to her friend's houses to "visit" and I get to go with her most of the time.

When we go to visit Mrs. Zimmermann, she always gives me a bottle of pop and a snack. And then I get to go down to their finished basement. A finished basement is a big deal. You've got to have some good money to make a nice family room in your basement. I love them because it's like a whole other private part of your house! The Zimmermann's kids are way older than me so there aren't a lot of toys to play with. But they've got one that I play with every single time. It's some kind of a game but I don't know how to play. There are a whole lot of plastic, pretend, Campbell's soup cans. I like to stack them in pyramids or pretend that I am working in a grocery store. I will set them up with other pretend grocery things and talk to my pretend customers as they shop. Sometimes I will even be the customer and talk to the pretend worker! When Mom is done visiting, she'll call me up. I quick clean it all up, thank Mrs. Zimmermann, and then we drive home so Mom can make dinner.

Visiting with Mrs. Olsen is my all-time favorite. Sometimes she comes to our house but her house is so magical. When you walk up the front steps, there is a first door that goes to the front porch. It is a front porch but it's really a room. There are windows, a TV, and shelves that are full of polar bears! Mrs. Olsen is what they call Norwegian. Her mom and dad are our friends too and we call them Deedy and Ragsie. They are as old as my grandparents but they are really different. I call my grandparents' Grandma or

Grandpa and then add their last name. My grandmas always wear dresses and sit on their couches. Deedy wears pants and sneakers and gives me great big hugs. Ragsie doesn't give hugs but he has a great, big smile. My parents told me that Ragsie was friends with the King of Norway. That's a big deal! Mrs. Olsen used to be an ice skater and was training to be on the U.S. Olympic figure skating team. I think that's why she has Barbie feet. She is barefoot a lot and when she crosses her legs, and one leg dangles, her foot is shaped EXACTLY like Barbie's. Once, when I was really little, Mrs. Olsen wasn't paying attention and I sat right down by her foot and ran my hand from her heel to her toes. She screamed, jumped in her seat, and her cigarette ashes fell right on my arm. But it didn't hurt and I had to check out her perfect foot!

If my mom isn't visiting with her friends at their houses, or visiting with her friends at our house, she is talking to her friends on the phone. She loves her friends and I love my mom. That means I love her friends, too!

The Playground

"Karen! The new playground is ready. Why don't you grab your friends and go check it out?"

Mom shouts up the stairs from the kitchen.

I sit up in my bed and gently lay down my latest Encyclopedia Brown mystery.

"It's ready?"

I grab my sneakers and race down the stairs, stopping on the landing to put my shoes on and tie my rainbow laces up tight in double knots. This is going to be an epic day and I can't stop again to bother with shoelaces. I jump the last two stairs and land solidly on both feet. As I turn to head out the back door, Mom stops me in my tracks.

"Have you eaten yet today?"

"No, not hungry, got to go!"

"Sit down and let me make you breakfast before you head out."

"Mah-ahm!"

"Sit."

I wait an agonizing two minutes while she prepares one of my favorite breakfasts, a strawberry Pop-Tart and orange Hi-C.

"You've got to take your allergy pill with some food."

I don't even need water, but I wait. Four little blue allergy pills a day go down easy for me, but that Pop-Tart is smelling delicious. I wait.

"Who are you going to play with today?"

"I'll grab Mary and Katherine, but who knows if Mary will come. I hate that she's two years older than me and thinks a lot of our games are dumb now."

"Maybe ring some bells at the end of the block—Stacy, Nan, Paul…"

Mom places my colorful breakfast in front of me.

"Well, I'll start with Mary and work my way down. Thanks for breakfast."

Is there anything better than ice cold Hi-C and a freshly toasted Pop-Tart? I think not. I am lucky my mom loves all this easy food to make and doesn't make me wait for oatmeal (blech!) or slimy eggs or something.

"I love you, Mom!"

After a quick hug, I'm out the back door and down the stairs in a flash. I take a right at the bottom of the driveway and cross the street to Mary's. I run to the back and knock on the door. Mary answers!

"Mary, hi! The new playground is done at Hatch! You wanna go play on it with me?"

"Not today. I've got a new magazine to read."

"But it's the new playground. It looks epic!!"

"Maybe another time."

She starts to close the door.

"Mary! Come ON! This will be fun. You can just hang out, you don't have to play anything, you can pick the game, you can be in charge, just please come with me."

I think she may actually be considering…

"Okay fine, but I'm too old to play so I'm going to just hang out. Let me tell my mom."

Within a few minutes, we are on our way. Our houses sit at the far end of Lenox Street and it's at the top of a great, big hill. So, we can't actually see the playground that now sits on the new blacktop of our school just at the other end of our block, down the hill, and across the very, very busy street of Ridgeland Avenue.

"Let's see if Katherine can come. And look, I know you both go to St. Giles, but Hatch is for every neighborhood kid. So you guys can totally play with all of it."

After a doorbell ring, a long wait, a few knocks, some looks in the window…we decide Katherine is not home and head down the street.

"My mom thinks we should invite Stacy, Nan, and Paul. What do you think?"

"Fine with me."

Mary is just not nearly as excited as I am.

As we head down the hill, everything comes into focus.

"Mary, do you see it? Do you see it???"

I can barely contain my excitement.

"Duh. Of course, I see it. Wow, it's a lot."

"It sure is! Forget the other kids, let's run!"

I take off, full speed ahead, and only stop when I get to the corner. Mary is still at least eight whole houses back.

"Mary, let's go!!"

Together we very, very carefully cross Ridgeland Avenue. Our whole lives we always had to stop at Mrs. Houghton's house and not go any further. Our parents always told us to come home when the streetlights came on, but we couldn't ever go down the hill. They always had to be able to come out to the front and look around to know where we were. They didn't care when, or if, we ate any meals, but we sure couldn't go down the hill. I've never even heard of a kid getting hit by a car on Ridgeland but our parents at the top of the hill sure weren't going to let it be their kids.

I stop in awe once I cross the sidewalk and make my way up the tiny hill to the new playground equipment at my beloved Hatch school. It takes a moment to take it all in.

There are three areas, and each area has long pieces of wood that look like railroad ties sectioning them off. Railroad ties! How cool is my school that we went to a railroad place for supplies! Then there is what someone called mulch all around the ground. It is like big chunks of softish wood. But not too big. I could hold a whole bunch in one hand.

But the best is the equipment. Each section is made for a certain age group. I am a big kid and am supposed to play on the biggest one. I stand at the bottom and just look up. There are bars and a tall ladder thing to get to the top. At the top is a fireman's pole. What on earth??? That looks terrifying and so very dangerous to me. Beyond the pole section is, well the best way I can describe it is that it is a wobbly bridge! More danger. You have to go past the death pole and brave the bridge to reach the biggest slide I've ever seen. And it has a wave in it! You slide partway down and then go forward and down the rest of the slide. It is magnificent and terrifying.

"Mary, do you see this?"

"Yeah, let's go," she screams as she runs to climb the mountainous structure.

"I'm good! I'll watch you," I yell at her.

"Chicken!"

"I'm no chicken," I yell. "That's just obviously not safe!"

She runs to the wobbly bridge. I cover my eyes. I hear her laughing as she jumps up and down. On the bridge that is not at all stable.

"Karen, get up here, this is so much fun! Don't be a chicken!"

She runs to the slide and is down in a flash all sweaty with excitement.

"Look, you made me come here. You've got to come up with me. You can do it."

"That's for the big kids and I don't think I'm as big as the kids who are supposed to play on it." I turn to the next smallest play zone and point. "I'll be here. This is for the medium kids and I'm a medium kid."

The medium kid area never looked better. It isn't quite as high, a little less death-defying, and has what will become one of my newest best friends…a tire swing! I run over and jump on.

"Mary, look at this! It smells amazing. Oh, I love the smell of hot rubber! And three chains…so shiny! Come over, let me give you a push."

I am swinging gently, pleading my case.

"I'll let you give me a ride, after you come on the big one with me."

What to do? I am drawn to the allure of the fresh tire swing and looking around, I see there is a tire swing in each play area. So cool! I don't want to play on the big structure, and I am no chicken. Ugh.

"Fine. Fine! I'm coming!"

I jump off the tire and quickly climb up the mammoth structure. I hold my breath as I skirt past the insane fire pole and make my way to the bridge. Mary is right behind me. I am stalled.

"Karen, go, GO! It's so fun!"

I can hear my heart beating in my ears, and it gets so loud that I can't hear Mary's voice anymore. I run across that bridge like a gazelle in the wild, just tearing across at breakneck speed. Whew. Then I am at the slide. My head feels spinny. This is obviously too dangerous for any sized children to be playing on. Am I up higher than the roof of the school building? I look over. No. No, I am not up that high, but it feels close! I can do this. I grab the bar and propel myself down. Wow is it fast! Mary is right behind me.

"Let's do it again! You've got to keep doing it so you won't be scared."

"You're nuts."

But the slide is exhilarating so I do it again. And again, and again. I even jump up and down on the bridge! I think I am laughing and Mary sure is. More neighborhood kids get word that the playground is ready, and the place is filling up.

"Mary let's get in line for the tire swing. I want to give you a ride!"

Let me explain the tire swing a little more. It isn't like the kind that hangs from a tree with a big rope. This is a fancy, playground tire swing. It is connected to a beam overhead by a big silver clip thing. Then three thick, silver chains are connected to that clip on one end, and then fan out down to three clips on the top of the tire. A single rider will sit down and put their feet into the opening across from them. Three smaller riders can fit with their feet either hanging down or tucked in between each other's bottoms. There are so many options.

The tire swing in the medium kid area becomes my domain. I establish myself as an expert tire-swing-ride-giver on that very first day. I don't know how it happens, but my technique develops, and word spreads. As time passes, you'll find me there before school, at class recess, lunch recess, and even after school. Not only do I have a tried-and-true technique for guaranteed fun, if I am in the right mood, I'll even sing for my riders. But not just any song. My go-to is I Will Survive by Gloria Gaynor. Because if you survive my ride, you become a bit of a legend yourself.

My first rider is Mary. Mary doesn't like to spin so I take it slow. I stand my ground and grab hold of the tire itself, one hand on two sections, spread evenly apart. I start by pushing her side to side and then progress to a slow, high circle. I am in the middle and totally in control of her fate. I pick up the speed and tell her to hold on.

I don't know how I know it, but my instincts take over. I grab the thick clip at the tire where the chain connects, and I spin that sucker just as hard as I can while I jump out of the way. Mary fights to hold on while screaming at the top of her lungs. Her feathered hair is slapping her in the face and flying backward all at the same time. And then she starts to laugh. She throws her head back and screams in delight! When she slows down, she takes a deep breath.

"That was awesome!"

As she goes flying on her second turn, other kids take notice. A line forms. My prowess as an expert tire-swing-ride-giver begins. But I don't add the serenading in for a while.

One day, it just happens:

My rider mounts the swing.

I tell them to tuck in their legs and hold on tight.

I stand in the center and start a gentle back and forth

I begin singing "I Will Survive."

I start slowly picking up speed.

The song continues, one line at a time.

Circular motion begins slowly.

Things speed up.

The excitement builds as the first spin hits the rider and my singing grows louder.

Back in for another build-up to a big spin.

For kids I don't know as well, the ride will end after two spins. There is usually a long line, and this makes perfect sense to me. If you are my friend, or if you are Tommy Swanson, you'll get the whole song. Is it fair? I think it is. The playground is my domain after all. I dominate kickball and am often asked to be the pitcher. I established myself as a fast runner back in first grade, and I am not afraid of the big kid, ginormous play structure anymore. What can't I do?

Well, for starters, I can't just go to the playground without permission because it is at the bottom of the crazy hill and across the very, very busy street. In time, I'll cross that bridge just like I crossed the wobbly bridge with Mary on the first day of play on the glorious Hatch School playground.

5th Grade

Being in 5th grade means having a classroom up on the third floor, near my PROBE room. My teacher is the lovely Mrs. Washington. She is from an exotic Caribbean locale and has a wonderful accent. She smiles a lot, and I can tell she really likes being a teacher. She is also great about me being in PROBE and I love having both of my classrooms on the same floor. I feel like such a big kid.

Mrs. Bennett's PROBE classroom is a special place. Now, as a 5th grader, it is important that I am kind to the younger kids. Mrs. Bennett tells me I am a leader, and I take that very seriously both in her classroom and Mrs. Washington's. In PROBE, we learn by units. We focus on one main topic and learn everything we can about it. We take field trips and write reports. My favorite units have been architecture, advertising, oil, and archaeology.

Once, on a field trip to Chicago to do an architectural tour, we take the EL (elevated train) into the city. While we are on the train, there is a mugging happening at one of the stops. Mrs. Bennett is brilliant and instructs all of us kids to look up at her while she shows us all how to hold our purses/bags so that it wouldn't be easy for a mugger to grab them.

Another field trip is an overnight trip with parent chaperones to the Dixon Mounds where we learn about archaeology up close at real burial mounds. I am most excited and impressed when our group studies advertising and gets to take the EL into the city again to sit in a real boardroom at the Leo Burnett Ad Agency. They are about to launch a brand new candy bar, the Whatchamacallit, and our class gets to each eat our very own candy bar as we help give the executives ideas.

I learn so very much from Mrs. Bennett and wow am I lucky she gets to be my teacher for four whole years. She gives the biggest hugs and she loves it when we ask her a question and she doesn't know the answer. We work together to try to find it out. I feel special and I feel smart.

5th grade feels like a big year. I get my green 10-speed Schwinn and I start babysitting and earning some real money.

Walking Towards Christmas

"David! Karen! Get down here! Time to go!"
Mom shouts from the bottom of the stairs.

"Coming!"

I look in the full-length mirror on the back of my door. Mom made my deep red, velvet dress and it's so beautiful. White tights, black patent leather shoes, and I'm ready for church. I love Christmas Eve!

Opening my door, I hear the creak of my brother's door as well. We race to the top of the stairs, and of course, he wins and gives me a gentle shove out of the way. He takes the stairs two at a time and I am following along, grateful the shove was gentle.

My dad tells us to hurry up and get our coats on.

"It's snowing outside, so grab your boots."

"No, please! I want to wear my shiny shoes. It's a special night!"

Mom chimes in, "Absolutely not! Both your shoes and your tights will get ruined in the snow. Grab your boots."

"But Mom, my boots are moon boots. They do NOT match the beautiful dress you made me. Pleeeease…"

"Karen Melissa, your mother said no. Get your boots, we don't want to be late!"

I take the five steps down to the basement landing and grab my silver and blue moon boots. They are great for playing in the snow, but not great for church on Christmas Eve. I pull them on and clomp back up the stairs where I spot my sister.

"Wait. Why does Sue get to wear her nice boots? Won't they get ruined?"

Sue is wearing her brown leather, zipper-up-the-side boots with chunky high heels.

"That's not fair!"

"Mind your own business and put your coat on. We need to go. NOW."

I bundle up, so angry that Sue gets to look so nice, and I look like I'm about to go on a space mission. David laughs right at me as he laces up his normal looking boots.

We head out the back door and carefully down the steps. Mom and Sue take the lead with Dad and David following behind. I'm on my own in the back making one giant leap for mankind. After walking across our very short backyard, we head to the shortcut.

All our garbage cans are back here and it's one of my favorite places. We turn left and follow the path until it veers right and suddenly, we're in the joint driveways of the Tanners and Smiths. Behind the Smith's garage isn't paved, and behind ours isn't either. They make the best hiding spots for night games in the summer, but in the winter it's just dead weeds and gunk. Unless it's snowing, and tonight it's snowing.

A thin layer of flakes dust the tops of the garbage cans and the driveways are just slick enough that we have to take our time and yet move quickly because it's Christmas Eve and all of the Chr-Easters will be in church and our spot might get taken. Dad says a Chr-Easter is a person who only comes to church twice a year—on Christmas and on Easter.

Have I told you about our spot? The Modder family absolutely has chosen the second pew from the front, on the right side, flush up against the aisle to the mid-point of the pew as our sacred space. No upstanding member of United Lutheran Church would dare sit in our spot. The Schmitt family sits directly in front of us in the first pew. I have no idea who sits behind us because I'm not allowed to turn around during church, unless we are sharing the peace, but I'm guessing every family has their self-assigned seats.

As we walk down the driveways Dad says, "No one should be in our seats. But it is Christmas Eve and everyone and their brother comes to church on Christmas Eve so someone just might get there and take our spot. Get a move on but be careful and don't slip."

Mom chimes in, "Most of this neighborhood is the Catholics so we should be okay."

At the end of the Tanner's driveway, we make a right-hand turn and I stop to take it in. It's late at night on Christmas Eve, snowflakes are falling gently, and up ahead is just the most magical sight. Christmas luminarias. My mom is instrumental in making sure all of the houses have their kits and magically, everyone, even the Catholics who go to St. Giles, set their bags out to light our way to church.

Luminarias are brown paper bags filled about halfway up with sand, and then you stick a thick candle in the middle, fold the sides down, and light the candles. The plan is to set them on both sides of your sidewalk, spaced out beautifully, to light our path as we walk to church at the very end of our block.

"It's so nice that everyone lights these for us."

I say this softly to myself. My brother hears.

"No moron, they aren't for us. Everyone, everywhere, lights these so Santa knows where to go."

"Well kids, they are just meant to be a festive decoration and people light them for their company and to make the block look nice for Christmas."

Whatever. I think they are just for us.

My sister and Mom step carefully in their heeled boots and I'm kind of glad for my moon boots. They are warm and keep me upright as I watch those two slide around and have to be held onto. I veer off the path and make footprints in people's yards as I look up and catch random snowflakes on my tongue.

"Karen Melissa, no dilly-dallying. Come on, we can't be late!"

I get back on the lit path and add a little Christmas skip to catch up. It's a short walk to church and soon we are there and the mood changes. We walk through the big wooden doors on the side of our church and stomp our feet on the red carpet with black trim in the entryway. Older ladies are sitting on the wooden pews on the sides, changing out of their boots into their dress shoes.

Mom, look! I could have done that! I could have brought my beautiful shoes."

"Next time. Let's get your coat hung up. Merry Christmas!"

She greets everyone with a big smile.

After we hang up our coats, we join the throng of people entering the sanctuary for the 11:00 service. What a smart time for a service! It ends at midnight the day Jesus was born. Smart! I'm ready to celebrate but keep my eyes on Dad's bald head. It's a good thing he's so tall, we can always find him in a crowd. He breaches the doors first and looks immediately to our row, turns, and nods with a big smile. Our seats are open! Yes!!

Church starts right at 11:00 with the ringing of the bells. I'm snuggled up against my mom in her green knit dress and bright red lipstick. She has the singing voice of an actual angel and I sing loudly to try to match her sounds. It makes her smile.

The best part of the service is the end when we all get candles to hold. Ushers come down the center aisle with the things to light the person on the end's candle. Then they light the candle of the person next to them. The whole church fills with a warm light as the overhead lights are turned off. We sing Silent Night, and it is magical. I am sleepy and so happy to be standing with my family in the warm light of Christmas.

MOXIE MATTERS

6th Grade

Sleepovers are my favorite social activity and really pick up in 6th grade. Ah, 6th grade. Finally, the oldest kids who get to rule the school. I am placed in Mr. Lawson's class. He is newer to the school so neither of my siblings had him. He has curly brown hair, a mustache, and a beard. He is on the shorter side and a bit round. His laugh is always straight from his belly and rolls out, filling up any space he is in. I love how he encourages his students to read and teaches us silly songs.

By 6th grade, I know pretty much everyone in my grade and am friends with them. My time at school is always positive. Since birdy Miss Jones in kindergarten, I've never gotten in trouble. I am even a helper in the office. Simply put, I love school.

Mr. Lawson is a good listener and somehow always seems to know what is going on with the 6th grade girl drama. I hate the 6th grade girl drama. I think I am friends with pretty much all the girls and the boys too. There is always talk about what girl got her period and for sure some of the girls are growing some boobs. Not me though. I am on the tall side, lanky, and flat as a board. I get teased a bit for that but not much because if a boy teases me, I just challenge him to a race at recess. I can outrun every single boy in my grade, except Randy "the Rocket" Arnett.

I don't love the drama that starts in 6th grade. Suddenly, not every girl is invited to a birthday party because now they are mostly slumber parties. As I am friendly with all the girls, I am invited to pretty much all of the slumber parties and I love them. I mean, I absolutely live for a good slumber party. I come with a plan, and pretty much every birthday girl appreciates my plan...or so I think.

Here's an outline of the plan: everyone arrives, we eat pizza and cupcakes, hang out, and as soon as things slow down, I introduce the idea that we all break into small groups and put on commercials. Everyone will agree and I'll go ahead and divide up all of the girls into small groups of 2-4. Then I write a bunch of product names down on slips of paper, fold them, and place them into a hat. We then spend time coming up with concepts, practicing, and then we perform for each other. It is So. Much. Fun. I really think everyone loves it. I then stay up all night long. I never go to sleep. I encourage others to stay up with me making up songs or skits or pranking anyone who falls asleep by dipping their hands in a bowl of cold, or warm, water to try to get them to pee their sleeping bags. Great fun. Until it isn't.

There is one clutch slumber party that I have to miss because we have a family party. I am sad to miss it, but these things happen. I'm sure they will still have a good time. The Monday morning after the party, something isn't quite right on the playground. No one will talk to me. The bell rings, and we file up to our classroom, and still, none of the girls will talk to me. Not one. I approach one friend after another, and they turn their back on me, or worse, pretend not to see me at all. With tears in my eyes, I turn to Mr. Lawson, who is taking it all in. He calls a meeting in the glass-enclosed pod room for every girl in the class, and it is mandatory.

Us girls make our way into the room, where all of the boys in our class, as well as Mrs. Mitchell's entire 6th grade class, can see us. This is what they see: every single girl, except for me, on one side of the room, Mr. Lawson in the middle, and me on the other side. Gulp. I am so confused. I also feel scared. Everybody is my friend. What is going on?

Mr. Lawson faces the pack.

"Ladies. What is going on?"

Crickets from them. Tears start rolling down my face.

"Ladies?"

One brave classmate speaks.

"Well, it's like this. She couldn't come to the slumber party this weekend and we all got to talking."

"Aaaand…"

Mr. Lawson prods.

"And we decided we don't like Karen always bossing us around. She always takes over the parties and tells us what to do and we don't like it."

I am stunned and the tears continue to flow. I thought people liked it when I helped move the party along. I thought it was appreciated. Oh boy. It is not. Everyone hates me. Oh boy. The tears are pouring from my eyes.

"Well ladies, it seems to me like it's important to tell Karen this, not give her the silent treatment. How can she know if no one is talking to her? Karen, do you hear what your friends are saying?"

"Yes. I didn't know. I thought I was helping, and everyone liked it."

"Karen, we usually do have fun, but we don't want you always taking charge and telling us what to do. If it's our party, we want to be in charge."

"Karen, do you hear what they are saying? Is there something you can do to make it better?"

"Yes Mr. Lawson, there is. I really am sorry everyone."

I wipe the snot on my sleeve.

"I just didn't know you don't like that."

Suddenly, a swarm of 6th grade girls converge in the middle of the pod room and Mr. Lawson throws up his hands and gets out of the way as the first group hug of my life happens amidst shouts of, "We love you, Karen" and "I'm so sorry everyone" and "You're so fun at parties" and "You are nice, just kind of bossy" erupts all around.

Sucking My Thumb

As a baby, I was gifted a light pink, quilted baby blanket with a satiny top. I think lambs were stitched into the front. The corners were rounded. I named her "Blankie."

Blankie went with me everywhere and was often held right up to my face, held tightly in my left hand with my thumb firmly in my mouth. As a little girl, I walked around without any shame at all, thumb in mouth, Blankie held tight.

I needed her to sleep and so she came with me on every vacation, overnight trip, and sleepovers to my cousin's. I openly adored Blankie and she was absolutely my nighttime companion. I could not sleep without her. She calmed me down if I fell and scraped my knee. I'd grip her to me, thumb in mouth, as Mom would sit me on the kitchen counter and put the orange mercurochrome on my owies. I'd dry my tears with her, and she always helped stop the pain.

When friends wouldn't want to play with me or play games my way, and I ended up alone in my room, I'd seek out Blankie to hold and comfort me. In the summer, I loved to hold Blankie up to the window unit air conditioner and get her super cold. The soft satin felt even better when she was cold.

If David wanted to watch a scary show or movie, he'd wait for me to go get Blankie. Once settled in, I'd pull her up to my face and insert my thumb.

As I got a little older, say mid-elementary years, Blankie was still my solid companion, but she didn't leave my room as much. Every night at bedtime though, I would greet her with glee and pull her close to me, left thumb in place.

At around this same time, the kids at school noticed the big callous on my left thumb. It sat on top of my knuckle, and I guess it was a little bit ugly. They'd ask what it was, and I would just shrug my shoulders and say something funny to get them to think about something else. I could usually make people laugh so this was effective.

In the wintertime especially, the callous on my thumb would crack and get a little bloody. But no problem, it would always feel better if I could just stick it back in my mouth a bit to soften it up. Sometimes I had to put a bandage on it. It was starting to become a little bit of a problem when I got to 4th, 5th, and then 6th grade.

My best friends know about Blankie, who by now has gotten so worn down and tattered that she is falling apart. So as pieces fall off, I just gently tie them on the end in a knot. At bedtime, I run my hands up and down, trying to find the smooth satin parts. My brother is starting to tell me Blankie is gross and stinks. Mom wants to clean her, but I am so afraid she'll fall apart.

One day, I carefully unknot all of her and lay the pieces out. I wash them all by hand using the small bottle of Woolite from the basement. They air dry and I do my best to tie them all back together. Not all of the pieces make it, and I save them in my underwear drawer. I still love her so and don't have the heart to throw any pieces away. I am never ashamed to bring her to a friend's sleepover, or to quietly suck my thumb when I think my friend is asleep.

The whole 6th grade class is going to White Pines Ranch for a sleepover field trip. My friend Debbie Barnes sits me down a few days before the trip.

"Karen, listen to me. You cannot bring your Blankie to White Pines. All of the girls are going to be sleeping on bunk beds in a big room. You cannot bring her. She might get lost. Other girls might make fun of you."

This feels like a blow to my spirit. I know, in my heart, that Blankie can't make the trip. I am growing up and sucking my thumb and loving my Blankie is for little kids. But I seriously do not know how I am going to fall asleep without her. Tears well up in my eyes.

"It's okay. I'll make sure I sleep right next to you. I'll help you fall asleep. You will be okay."

"Okay, Debbie. I trust you. Thank you."

The first night at White Pines, all of the girls climb into their bunks. I hold my left thumb up really close to my face but don't put it in my mouth.

I whisper to Debbie, "I'm scared. I don't think I can do this."

Debbie then stands up and walks over to my bed, holding her satin robe in her hands.

"I brought this as backup. You can snuggle with this. It should feel like your Blankie. Just don't stick your thumb in your mouth. No one will know."

I hold her robe close and for the first time in my memory, I sleep without sucking my thumb.

This is a true friend.

6th Grade Talent Show

A brilliant idea comes to me. I approach Hatch Elementary School's music teacher, the kind-hearted, show-loving Mrs. Coffman. Mrs. Coffman is young and has a beautiful head of curly, pale red hair. Mom says she is a hippie with her flowy skirts and unmake-upped face.

Earlier in this sixth-grade year, she directed both Mr. Lawson's and Mrs. Mitchell's classes as we sang Don't Fence Me In as a background for an actual documentary that would be featured on TV or something. I certainly make sure to always be on her good side, just in case there are any more performance opportunities on my horizon.

I arrive at the music room before school starts one day and pitch my idea. The sixth grade should perform a talent show for the entire school and all the parents! Won't it be wonderful to fill the auditorium, maybe even sell tickets, and share all our talents with the greater Hatch community?

She agrees to the sixth graders from my class performing for the sixth graders in Mrs. Mitchell's class. Well…it is something at least and she puts me in charge of not only directing the show but producing it as well. Dreams become reality in my twelve-year-old life. This is the big time. My last big actual stage role in second grade as a fortune teller at the school circus paled in comparison to the possibilities of what could be with this talent show.

Where to begin? I work hard to convince my classmates to create acts showcasing their talents. I start with my maybe boyfriend, Tommy Swanson. I think for sure he can do magic or something.

"No way, but you go ahead and do it!"

That's encouraging! He doesn't want to perform but he thinks I should. Exciting! I approach my classmates face-to-face at recess, before school, after school, and I even wrote notes inviting them to perform. I got a lot of, "What? No! You do it." And some, "Are you crazy?" Well, guess what, I am going to do it and no, I am not crazy. Gheesh. While no one is interested, at least they are supportive of my contributions. I finally get two acts added to my own three acts making five total.

We have a show!

My time becomes consumed with hand drawing programs on folded construction paper and checking in with the other two acts to make sure they are rehearsing and ready for the big day. I barely rehearse my three acts which is totally fine because I am used to performing on the fly and throwing down a quick costume change behind the evergreens.

The school administration won't allow us to use the auditorium and stage and that, of course, becomes a major disappointment to this performer. I crave redemption on the big stage after the debacle of my third-grade Brownie bridging ceremony.

My hope for stage redemption is smushed like a lightning bug on the sidewalk in summer on the bottom of my older brother's shoe. But I will not let my light burn out! Instead, the talent show will be performed at the front of the music classroom. Disappointing for sure, but workable.

I arrive early at school the day of the show so I can set up the room. I decide to have the audience sit on the carpet squares on the floor, facing the makeshift stage. I carefully place all my costumes and props to the side of the stage area on the windowsill. Thirty minutes before showtime, all the acts are excused from class to go and prepare. I tell Mr. Lawson I should go sooner because I am the Director. He does not agree. Once out of my classroom and descending the stairs from the third floor to the first, I do some deep breathing to calm my racing heart. Confidence and excitement pulse through my veins.

I stop in the bathroom to change into my first costume, a pale lavender leotard and white tights. As I brush my hair back into a tight, high ponytail, I calm any bubbling nerves by reminding myself that I am a performer and I have been a performer my whole life.

It is time.

Mrs. Coffman introduces me to begin the show. I thank everyone for coming, instruct them to follow along in their handmade programs, and to please enjoy the show. I will open the show with an improvised dance to the song Open Arms by the brilliant band Journey. I take my place in front of the entire sixth grade and as the music starts, I take a deep breath, and literally make up movements to mirror the lyrics of the song:

I lay down on my side.

I cover my eyes with my hand.

I jump up and pulse my hand on my heart.

I point to myself.

The dance continues for the entirety of the song. All three minutes and seventeen seconds. There is no fear as I become a pioneer in the interpretive dance movement. It does not matter that the only dance training I had was when I was five years old at Miss Rose's Dance Academy. It does not matter because I become one with the song. As I dance, I notice Tommy Swanson staring at me, eyes wide, mouth open aside from the occasional smacking of his gum. I also notice our principal, Mr. Donaldson, quietly stepping into the back of the room. His smile so big that he has to cover it with his hand.

What a day!

Once the song ends, I feel an indescribable exhilaration as I introduce the next act and then discreetly move to the side of the stage by the windowsill. I nonchalantly pull up a skirt over my leotard and tights and slide on a pair of clogs. I stand tall in support of my classmate as they are talking through a science experiment of some sort. My heart is beating so fast, and it pounds in my ears, making it almost impossible to hear anything.

I have a big smile plastered to my face as the Host of the big show. I take some more deep breaths, but no one can tell because I use the tricks I learned from my ventriloquism kit that I received from Santa this year. I keep my teeth together and take measured breaths, never breaking the bright smile that Mrs. O'Rourke always told me she loved.

As the science act concludes, I clap my castmate off the stage and I invite my friend Shannon up for my, our, next act. This is going to be a doozy and a crowd pleaser for sure. I take my right hand and hold Shannon's left as we sing a duet of the popular song Ebony and Ivory by Paul McCartney featuring Stevie Wonder. Shannon and I practiced once or twice at recess. We are more than ready.

Mrs. Coffman starts the cassette tape recording of the song, and we sing along in what might be the most groundbreaking performance the music room has ever seen. Shannon and I glance at each other and then the audience, all smiles as we serenade our peers with Paul and Stevie quietly accompanying us as we belt our voices over theirs.

What a thrill! Almost everyone in the room claps. Mrs. Coffman has to shush a few talkers during the performance, but we hardly notice from our vantage point in the spotlight. After a bow, or two, Shannon returns to her seat on the floor and I introduce the next act and sidestep my way to my costume/prop area to prepare for my final performance, the last act of the show. I slowly slide on my fancy vest while keeping my big smile and ventriloquist breathing in check so as not to disturb the trumpet solo the audience is eagerly consuming. Mr. Donaldson seems to be thoroughly enjoying himself as he keeps rubbing his ears to make sure he can hear alright. I check to make sure my props are loaded and ready to go as my classmate wraps their number with some big notes.

I lead the musician to their seat on the floor and give my final speech of the day before my closing number.

"Friends, classmates, teachers, and Mr. Donaldson, I want to thank you all so very much for coming today and for supporting the arts. Without further ado, I am proud to share our finale with you now…"

It is time for my biggest number, my comedy act to the song I Love a Rainy Night by Eddie Rabbitt. Mrs. Coffman loads the cassette into the player, gives me a big thumbs up, and I sing along with Eddie. Whenever we sing the word "rainy" I douse my audience with water from various items loaded prior to the show. It is a hit! People are laughing! Tommy Swanson gives me a surprised look that I find endearing when I shoot him right in the eye with a squirt gun. He loves it. Mrs. Coffman stands up and starts circling the room. I'm sure she is planning a way to thank me for all my hard work, and it has nothing to do with a few of the girls who start screaming because their hair is getting wet. There is a lot of laughter.

The song ends and I take my final bow. I invite the other acts and my duet partner up to the stage with me. As we bow together, I can't help but gush at the triumph of the show. I was born for this stuff; I just know it. Mr. Donaldson approaches me after the show.

"Miss Modder, you've got moxie, you really do."

I am not sure what moxie means, but I am pretty sure it has to do with talent.

Summer, 1982

Saturday morning. Or is it afternoon?

I wake up and do a big stretch. Rolling over, I see the sun blasting behind my green blinds. My alarm clock says 11:17. Excellent! I've slept long enough that I can now have lunch for breakfast. I take my time getting out of bed and grab my favorite pair of blue terry cloth shorts with the two white ribbon stripes on each side. I find the matching top smushed in my dresser drawer. My white sweat socks with the blue stripes at the top are dirty and laying on my floor but what the heck? They match and are perfect for my afternoon plans. I pull them up to just below my knee and check myself out in the mirror on the back of my door. My hair! What style today? I give it a good brush and choose a high, side ponytail. My look is coming together!

Grabbing my Walkman and favorite cassette, I head to the hallway. Glancing left, I see the bathroom and make a quick pit stop. I run my tongue over my teeth and think about whether or not they need to be brushed. Might as well! A quick squirt of Crest onto my toothbrush and then I'm headed downstairs for breakfast/lunch—oh wait, that's brunch!

Mom is down in the basement, probably doing laundry. David is playing Atari in the TV room, and no one else is around. I open the fridge and grab my favorite Saturday breakfast, cold pizza, and a cold Pepsi. Every Friday night we get Amato's pizza and I love it so much. Just cheese for me and I like it that way. No one else likes plain cheese so I get my own pizza and the leftovers are all mine.

I grab the bottle opener from the silverware drawer and pop the top off my Pepsi. Best meal ever! I finish up and Mom is coming up the basement stairs.

"Karen, it's about time you woke up. What are your plans for the day?"

"I was up late reading, Mom. Reading is good for me! It looks like a perfect day to roller skate. So, I'm going to lace up my skates and hit the streets in a few."

"Stick to the sidewalks. The streets aren't as safe."

"Mom, the sidewalks aren't smooth. I need a smooth surface to get my moves down. Don't worry, I'll be careful."

"Okay, maybe skate over to a friend's house or something."

"Nah, I'm cool just skating with my jams."

I hold up my cherished Walkman and grin. Then I get my skates from the basement landing and peek in at my brother.

"Wow! You're so good at Asteroids. Will you teach me how to get better?"

"No."

"Please! I'll do anything!"

"No."

"Mo-om, David won't help me get better at Asteroids. Make him!"

"David, teach your sister."

"No."

"Asteroids is stupid anyway. I'm going to skate!"

I head out the back door and down to the second-to-the-bottom step where I sit and lace up my matching-to-my-outfit blue, gym shoe, roller skates. They're a velvety blue with white stripes down the sides and a gorgeous yellow stopper on the front. I stand up and do a spin with my arms out. Looking up at the blue skies, I just know it's going to be an amazing day.

Adjusting my headphones on my ears, I clip my Walkman to the waist of my shorts and hit play as I skate down the driveway. Just one thing could make this day better…please God, let him appear…please…God…I'm almost to the end of the driveway and there he is, in all of his skating glory.

Directly across the street and two doors to the left skating down the newly blacktopped driveway is the one, the only, Kent

Madison. Yessss! Tall, blonde, longish feathered hair, thin-but-kind-of-muscley, wearing short satin shorts and matching sweat socks just like mine, boombox ON HIS SHOULDER, and NO SHIRT, is the much older, but maybe still a teenager...Kent Madison. I stand at the foot of my driveway, hoping he will turn left at the bottom of his and skate over. Maybe he'll invite me to skate with him! I do a little dance in place, holding my breath.

Nope. Perfect Kent Madison turned right and skated down Lenox Street, to the beat of his music—some kind of disco, like the best roller skater I have ever seen in my life. He is the greatest. Maybe he'll see me next time and we can skate together. I'm not in love with him or anything. Gross. He's super old. I just am in love with his rhythm on skates.

I turn my tape on, pump up the volume and decide to skate to the right. Kent went the other way and that's a pretty big downhill that ends at a busy street. I don't think I'm ready for that route quite yet. I breathe in and start to feel the wind in my side pony as Safety Dance blasts in my ears. I get skating to the beat and find myself weaving all around the neighborhood, on the street. I don't have a care in the world. It feels wonderful.

MOXIE METER

Mom

If someone was to ask me where Mom is, there are three places that come to mind.

Maybe her favorite place in our home is sitting at the little desk alcove in our kitchen. Our kitchen table was built into the wall with a pedestal stand below. It is round but branches out with a little desk area that is small, but gets the job done. Our golden yellow telephone hangs on the wall, with the stick-on, shoulder-resting attachment stuck to it. This allows long conversations to be much more comfortable. There are two mugs, a guy and a gal, meant to represent my parents. They are filled with pens, pencils, and the ever-important emery board. My mom has notebooks stacked to the left and the family calendar can be found here as well. My sister and brother made paper-holding gadgets in junior high woodworking and one of these hangs next to the phone. If we answer the phone and have to take a message, the handy paper roll hangs right there.

My mom doesn't have a job outside of raising us kids. She is a passionate volunteer though, and that keeps her very busy. She volunteers at church, specifically redecorating the large room and library found off the fellowship hall on the first floor. That was a big and exciting project for her, and she really seemed to enjoy it. She also volunteers for the Infant Welfare Society and loved when she was President and ran the A.S.I.D. Showcase House.

I remember tagging along to the big, fancy homes throughout all stages of readiness for the big event. A local home is chosen each year and then interior decorators are given a room to decorate and the culmination is selling tickets to the community and raising money for the programs Infant Welfare supports. There is always a gift shop in the basement or garage of the home, filled with homemade treasures from the women in the greater organization. I love it when my mom is the President/Chairwoman because I can wander the house and put my imagination to the test. If only Jonathan and Jennifer Hart were allowed to let loose to solve a mystery or two!

One year, my brother was the hired caretaker and got to live in the house! He was in college then and while I thought it was magical, I got the impression he thought it was creepy and slightly annoying to have to deal with all the people coming and going. Infant Welfare hosts other events throughout the year as well. There is a big brunch with a theme and one year my mom was in charge and the theme was Ports of Call. We borrowed an authentic Norwegian costume/dress from Mrs. Olsen, my mom's best friend. The local paper sent a photographer to our house, and they took pictures of me in the dress and my mom adjusting my headpiece. It made me feel special to wear the outfit and especially to pose with my mom in an actual newspaper! We laughed as the pictures were being taken and the photographer asked about our Norwegian heritage. These two blondes don't have a drop of Norwegian blood in us, but we giggled and said how much we loved it.

Barbara Modder of Oak Park adjusts the headdress worn by her daughter Karen who will model the costume at the 14th "Port-of-Call" March 13. (Staff photo by Geoff Scheerer)

14th 'Port-of-Call' is Norway

Circle 1 of Oak Park-River Forest Infant Welfare Society will present its 14th "Port-of-Call" benefit at 12:30 p.m. March 13 in the Kimberly Room of Nielsen's Restaurant, 7330 North Av., Elmwood Park.

This year's port-of-call is Norway, land of the midnight sun.

According to co-chairmen Carol Capps and Barbara Jepsen, guests may wear costumes of the country to the Sunday brunch.

Among those who'll dress for the occasion is Karen Modder, daughter of Barbara Modder, president of the local Infant Welfare Society and a member of Circle 1.

Karen's costume comes from the Hardanger region of Norway. It is the same as those worn by Norwegian women when they attend weddings, funerals, holiday celebrations or any event where guests are honored.

Cost of reservations is $16. Deadline is March 11.

For informaton or reservations, call Jepsen, 848-6002.

My mom is committed to another organization that really benefits children. She attends meetings, spends lots of time on the phone, and helped create a shelter for the most vulnerable children in the Chicagoland area. As a member of the Board, she gives so much effort to help provide a safe space for kids to live when their lives are often destroyed by violence, extreme abuse, and neglect.

Both of my parents set a strong example of working for the betterment of our community. My dad served on the local Community Chest board, and our Church Council. I admire that they both work to make the lives of kids better and I'm not sure where that drive comes from. I do know that it sets a wonderful example for me to follow when I'm an adult.

Besides the kitchen table nook that houses her office and the telephone, Mom, on most afternoons, is in her bedroom. She likes to take a nap. Everyone in the house knows when it is her nap time so we must be very quiet. She heads to her room, turns on the TV, and lays down. I never understand why she is so tired. What does she even do besides sit on the phone, file her nails, write things down, do laundry, get the house picked up for the cleaning lady who comes every other Saturday, cook us our meals, volunteer, and shop…?

At night, after dinner at promptly 6:15, Mom will usually sit at the kitchen table for a while and smoke while my sister or I clean up the dishes. Then she sometimes watches TV with us in the TV room, but mostly she watches her shows on the little color TV in her bedroom.

As nights wear on, when it is always very dark, I can look from the kitchen, through the hallway and dining room and into the front room and see the orange glow of her lit cigarette gliding back and forth at a slow pace. As a little girl, I would go and investigate this floating orange light and find my mom, with a record playing quietly on the record player, walking back and forth. There was always an ashtray on the fake fireplace mantle where she'd flick her ashes and sometimes, I bet her thoughts as well. Usually, she was sweet and told me she was thinking and to leave her alone. Occasionally, she'd stop and put up a hand before I even got to the living room and would tell me to go. Once in a while, my dad would see me facing her pacing and intercept me before I could walk towards her. This was her thinking time, and eventually, I stopped even trying to join her.

I wanted to walk with her. To hold her hand and help her think.

MOXIE MATTERS

Earning Sticker Money

The Gilmores live out the back door, through the shortcut, and down the block halfway. Kevin Gilmore is a new baby and he's so, so cute! I babysit him while his mom runs quick errands during the day. I love dressing him up in all of his baby clothes. He's just like a doll! Mrs. Gilmore always has him taking a nap when I get there. She doesn't know that I wake him up a little while later and change his clothes a few times before putting him back in his crib. Then she lets me stay and play with him after she gets back. I'm so lucky!

A hard babysitting job is right across the street for the Browns. They have three sons, and their oldest son is just a little bit younger than me. He has Down Syndrome. I think he has some other things that are going on too. He is always sitting on his beanbag chair watching TV when I come over. The other boys are a handful and so busy. Mrs. Brown only pays me $.50 an hour. That's nothing for three kids who I really need to keep an eye on. And even though they pay so low, Mom tells me I have to scrub their house clean while I'm there. I don't think it's fair, but Mom says Mrs. Brown needs help and I'm the one to do it. I ask Mom if she wants to walk across the street and clean while I babysit. She tells me to watch my "smart mouth."

"Why? Is it going to do tricks?"

Then I get sent up to my room. But that's not really a punishment because I love my room.

The other family I babysit a lot for is the Turners. I can walk to their house too! So much for needing my 10-speed to get to work. The Turners have a little daughter named Melissa. My middle name is Melissa so I think we are connected in some way. She was my sister's favorite client before my sister got too cool to babysit. The Turners have kind of a modern house with a cool TV center that is all glass shelves and cabinets that cover the whole wall. Their TV is ginormous and they have cable.

I like it when Melissa goes to bed, and I can watch movies on HBO and Showtime. I even watch R-rated movies that my parents would never let me see, and I get PAID for it! One night while I am watching cable TV at their house and Melissa is tucked up in bed, I see some magazines on the glass top coffee table. I start picking them up to look through them and see it. Playboy. I am so creeped out. I know what Playboy magazine is because Mary's older brothers hide them up in their attic and she showed us once when we were having a Charlie's Angels adventure in her house.

Playboy magazine scares me because it is filthy and I wasn't ever supposed to look at one. Why did the nice, quiet Turners have a filthy magazine? My heart starts to race as I carefully put all of the magazines back exactly where they were, covering the filthy Playboy. When they get home from being out, Mr. Turner is going to walk me home but I am scared of him now.

"No, thank you."

Then I run all the way home. I don't know what to do about the Turners. They pay $5 an hour and I get good snacks and free cable. But I am so creeped out by the magazine. I don't even know who to turn to for advice on this one.

The next morning, I call Mary. Because she is two years older than me, she pretty much knows everything.

"Mary, I was babysitting for little Melissa down the street last night. I found a Playboy. A Playboy! I don't know what to do. Now I'm afraid of Mr. Turner. Isn't it creepy?"

"Are you afraid of my brothers?"

"Well yes, but not because of the magazines hiding in your attic."

"It's dumb to be afraid of Mr. Turner. I'm sure they get it for the articles. That is why my dad said most people get it."

"Okay, you're right. And they pay good money, and the kid is cute."

"Stop freaking out."

"Okay. Thanks! Bye."

I hang up with Mary. Gosh, it's good to have an older and wiser friend.

Stickers

My sticker collection rivals anyone's I know. Probably because it is on display for all to see...on my bedroom door.

It started off innocent enough. I placed one sticker on the door to cover up a small flaw in the woodwork. It made me smile. Over time, I realized that my parents never actually ventured to the second floor of our home, so I got brazen and added more stickers, one at a time.

A lot of my friends have actual sticker-in-books collections but what is the point of that? Why collect such art if I can't enjoy them on the regular? So, one at a time, the collection grows. Soon my goal is to cover the entire door with stickers.

Some might wonder what drew me to this style of art expression. I think it simply traces back to when I was a really little kid and excellent work was rewarded with a sticker. And not just any sticker would do. The prize of all young kids back in that day was the coveted scratch-n-sniff sticker. I still love a good scratch-n-sniff, especially pizza or strawberry!

I don't know where my teachers have bought them. I sure can't find them in stores, and not even the Service Merchandise catalog which has absolutely everything cool under the sun.

What would guarantee me a scratch-n-sniff? For sure a 100% on the Friday spelling test and definitely when I would show mastery of my times tables. Once in a blue moon, a scratch-n-sniffer will be applied to excellent cursive handwriting. Do teachers even know this is why I am such an excellent student? It is all due to the appeal of banana, bubble gum, strawberry, and the granddaddy of them all—chocolate cake.

Do other sniffing sensations tantalize us kids of the late '70s and early '80s? Absolutely. My first scent-sational quest was to work with rubber cement. When a teacher would put out a project with the little brown bottles lined up alongside, us kids thought we hit the jackpot. We were never allowed our own bottles of rubber cement and for good reason. Every kid literally got lost in the light-headedness of a deep inhale after opening the jar.

Somehow rubber cement is replaced by plain old Elmer's glue as we get older and well, no good smells from that thin, white liquid. My brother and I will absolutely cover a single hand in a full layer of glue for the sole reason of watching it dry and then peeling it off. Are there any benefits? Do we have softer skin like when my mom melts paraffin and sticks her hands in the pot? Nope. It is just super fun. (But not quite as fun as anything to do with Silly Putty.)

In 5th and 6th grade for sure, the smelly goal was a set of scented markers. My sister scored some and it was all I wanted for myself. Each color matched an actual smell of the same color. Genius! Blue was blueberry. Who knew blueberries even had a smell? Not this girl. The markers smelled amazing when you opened the cap and carefully brought it straight to the nostril. There was an initial smell when you used it on paper, but nothing that lasted. I tried. I was definitely disappointed when my fruit salad concept failed on paper. Yellow smelling banana, red strawberry, blue blueberry, and so on.

My sticker collection is born from my absolute fascination with scratch-n-sniff wonders shared by my hard work in school. I buy most of my stickers at either Logo's Books or Foster's Toys. They are displayed on a turning column of brightness and joy. Most stickers are packaged in large rolls that hang on the column. A large sticker will fill an entire 2x2" waxy square. Medium stickers might include 2-4 on a square. The smallest of stickers, your hearts, smiley faces, and so on, fill the entire space. Such a great bang for your buck as Dad would say.

My favorite stickers include anything rainbow. Holographic rainbows blow my mind. 3D rainbows? You can bet your sweet patootie they are in my collection. The Izod alligator? Yes please, in all the sizes. Trees, flowers, leaves, smileys, all of it, yes please.

Allowance money, babysitting money, birthday, Christmas, finding coins around the house…they all feed my need to fully and completely cover my bedroom door with the goodness and joy that are stickers. Once the interior is adequately filled, I start on the perimeter.

Over the years, my interest has waned just a little bit. As I grow up, I am always on the lookout for a unique sticker to adorn my door. The collection never ends although I think it is all over one day when Dad suddenly appears in my room. He is a little sweaty and his bald head is a little bright red.

"What on earth have you done to your door?"

His voice is very controlled while pointing at my masterpiece.

"That's my sticker collection. You've seen me buying them."

"But we never told you to put them ON YOUR DOOR!"

"You never told me not to."

"Karen Melissa, you will scrape every last one of these stickers off of this door!"

"Dad, no! This is worth so much money! Look at how amazing they are. And so much money. Please. How about when we move someday, I can then remove them all?"

He looks at me. He looks at my prized collection. He looks at me again.

"Fine. Fine. But no more. Do you hear me? No more!"

I jump up and gave him a big hug.

"I hear you!"

Of course, that doesn't mean I will do what I heard. The collection continues to grow, and he is never any wiser. Mostly because I don't think he ever came upstairs again.

Junior High

When junior high rolls around, I make so many new friends and love it. Birthday parties are a thing of the past, we are too old and too cool for them now. But small group friend sleepovers or one-on-one sleepovers become the core of my social life.

While some shenanigans started in the 6th grade sleepovers, junior high is time for some serious terror and lots of shenanigans.

"Light as a feather, stiff as a board. I'm going to tell you the story of the night you died…"

Finger Lifting. The focus of most every group sleepover. I love being the Storyteller. My role is to sit at the head of the chosen victim, er, um volunteer. She lays on her back, arms at her sides, muscles tight. Other girls sit on either side of her and place their index and middle fingers, also taut, just underneath the victim/volunteer's body.

The Storyteller starts with, "Light as a feather, stiff as a board. I'm going to tell you the story of the night you died…" and then I create a horrific tale. Once finished, the Storyteller adds her strong fingers under the girl's shoulders, and all of the girls chant together, "Light as a feather, stiff as a board, light as a feather, stiff as a board…" As we lift the girl up high into the air.

It is some kind of crazy, voodoo magic that works every single time. In our minds, the spirit world comes and helps us lift this hypnotized girl way up high.

Oh, there are times it doesn't work. And it is always, always because the girl fidgets, or maybe she doesn't concentrate or believe in the story enough. It is always her fault, never the Storyteller's.

Beyond Finger Lifting, we always try the old put-the-newly-asleep-girl's-hand-in-a-bowl-of-warm-water to get her to pee her pants. Or is it supposed to be cold water? We never know which is right and I'm sure that's why it never actually works.

Telling scary stories, watching scary movies if the girl has cable, an occasional Ouija board experience, these are all on the scary track.

But some sleepovers are for hijinks and hilarity. On these occasions, I have a full arsenal of things to suggest. And note, I learned my lesson in 6th grade and always approach a sleepover host cautiously. That means I mostly still convince her my ideas are great, or I just host a whole lot of sleepovers.

Prank calls are the absolute best fun at the time. There is no way to know who is calling. It is thrilling!

For prank calls, we grab a phone book and pick a random number to call. Then we say the goofiest things when the person answers. My favorite is to just pretend. Pretend to be a salesperson, a long-lost family member, a jilted girlfriend. But those can turn dark quickly so we mostly stick to the scripts:

"Is your refrigerator running? You'd better go and catch it!"

Hang up. Laugh hysterically. We use this same line over and over again. Once in a while, we might call someone and tell them they've won a prize and then set up delivery. I love prank calls.

One sleepover idea that my junior high friends and I really have fun with is the Commercials game. I think I made it up back in elementary school, but I don't want to come across as bossy again, so I'll share the credit. This works best with a larger group of sleepover friends and ends up finding its way to simple nights in with friends.

Oh, the fun of sleepovers!!

In 8th grade, one of my elementary school pals and I decide to co-host a Halloween sleepover at her house. Costumes are a must and Lisa and I actually rent ours. We wear matching old-timey bathing costumes with cute little hats and everything. We buy all kinds of decorations, and my favorite is fake spider webs. We wrap that stuff all over her living room and set a pretty spooky scene.

This feels like an important party because it is a combo of invites for both of us. Hatch school friends combined with new Emerson Jr. High friends. Not everyone knows each other well. We are a little nervous about that. Everyone shows up in costumes ranging from Charlie Chaplin to Dorothy from The Wizard of Oz.

The night gets underway with scary stories, some finger lifting for old time's sake, a few commercials, and a rousing game of freeze dance to my special Halloween album featuring Monster Mash. Soon it is time to settle down in the basement and let some of the girls fall asleep.

Lisa's basement is unfinished but in good shape because her dad leads church down there. The floors and walls are painted red and that gives me some pause. On Halloween, it adds a layer of creepy that is just right in my opinion. Sleeping bags are unfurled and some girls change into their pajamas. But not everyone changes. I explain that it is pajama time but some girls just giggle and shake their heads.

What is happening? We are the hosts, and the guests are seeming to rebel here. One of the girls speaks up.

"We're waiting for Lisa's parents to go to bed and then we are going to sneak out and teepee!"

What?!?! This is not in the plans and certainly against the rules. You'd think with all of my prank calling tucked away, I am a big rule breaker. I am not. The idea of people sneaking out causes me to break out into a serious sweat.

Lisa speaks up, and I am so glad she is going to set them straight.

"Yea, let's do it!"

Everyone, except me, thinks that sounds like fun. I refuse. Sneaking out? On Halloween? Breaking the rules? Tee-peeing people's houses? No, thank you.

It appears Lisa's parents went up to bed. All lights are turned off and everyone starts putting their shoes on to hit the 'hood with their mayhem. I put on my pajamas and snuggle into my sleeping bag. I am teased a bit but just say I am very tired. They head up the basement stairs as I try to get comfortable on the red, cement floor.

They tiptoe up the stairs. I try to calm my racing heart. I am so afraid they'll get caught, arrested even.

Suddenly, I hear the rumble of feet charging back down the stairs. As I slowly lift my head off my pillow, I look up and see a single, ruby red slipper, right as it comes crashing down on my head. My head does a bit of a slam and bounce as the lights are flicked on.

The girls are all sliding into their sleeping bags, as fast as they can, fully dressed, and immediately pretend to be asleep.

I am seeing double and feel like I am going to throw up. What just happened?

After a moment, everyone seems to exhale at the same time.

"Wow, that was close!"

"We almost got caught!"

"I can't believe your mom came back downstairs!"

I don't feel well and start to cry as I slowly sit up, looking at these hooligans.

"Dorothy stepped on my head when you came running back down! She stepped on my head, and I don't feel right! I'm really scared. Someone call my dad!"

A few minutes later, my dad is picking me up and taking me home. He calls our pediatrician who tells him it sounds like I have a concussion and need to stay awake the rest of the night.

Concussed by a rogue Dorothy and her band of would-be tee-pee-ers.

Mr. Mom

Our basement is also unfinished and a little rough around the edges. It was one of my favorite places to play as a kid and now to hide out as pre-teen. Our bonafide gymnastics mat is no longer under the ping pong table for my childish games. Now it's out in the middle of the basement.

Back when I was a little kid, in fifth and sixth grade, I loved all-things gymnastics. The pommel horse, the uneven bars, the rings, the balance beam, and the floor mats. We did a unit in 6th grade PE and it was a dream for me. Our two PE teachers were both gray-haired, a man and a woman. I think his name was Mr. Crawford. He was tall, kind of pear-shaped, and mostly crabby. She was tiny, tightly curled hair, and I don't ever remember a smile on her face.

We had Mr. Crawford for our 6th grade gymnastics unit and when the gym doors opened and we walked in to see all of the equipment out, I lit up like our artificial Christmas tree. My flexibility was a bit of a surprise given my above-average height. For the first few days of gym, we learned each of the stations. The vault was my favorite because I was a fast runner and could easily do the squat-through or even better, the straddle-over. I was nervous about a handspring over but knew with practice that I'd get there.

The uneven bars were fun, and the smell of chalk made my senses tingle. I loved the freedom of swinging and switching bars. The beam—not my strength. My ingrained fear of heights made this piece of equipment my biggest challenge. The rings involved more chalk, flexibility, and swinging so I loved them. But the floor, well, that was my favorite. Walkovers (front and back), round-offs, limbers, sitting in the splits, and maybe my favorite ever…a dive roll.

Once we had all of the stations down and safety measures were memorized, we were free to rotate between each station. I Love Rock and Roll became my anthem as I breezed through them full of confidence.

At home, my sister's gym mat in the basement became a favorite place of mine and where I was one night in eighth grade when the phone rang.

My radio is tuned into B96 and I am determined to get my front walk-over back again. Hands over head, right toe forward, point the toe, step into handstand, bend over forward, one leg at a time...Shoot! I keep getting stuck in the handstand and nervous about going forward. Try again. Try again. Try again.

"Karen!"

Mom yells down the basement stairs.

"Telephone!"

A phone call! For me! I thought for sure my day was going to be spent nailing this move. Who could it be? I skip over to the bottom of the stairs.

"Coming!"

"Don't be long, I'm waiting for a call."

"Hello?"

"Hi Karen, it's Veronica!"

Veronica Mooney!

"Hi Veronica!"

"So, a group of us are going to see Mr. Mom tonight at the Lake Theater. Do you want to come?"

Any saliva in my throat completely dries up. Veronica Mooney is so nice, so beautiful, so popular. And she is inviting me to the movies??? Without hesitation, I respond.

"Yes! Yes! I'd love to go to the movies with everyone."

I dared my next question.

"Who all is going?"

"Oh, the whole gang. Dina, Cindy, Roseanne, Gretchen, you know, everybody."

And ME. I am invited to join the popular girls at the movies. In public. Tonight!

We hang up with the plan to meet in front of the Lake Theater fifteen minutes before the movie starts. My parents are thrilled that I have plans. They go out practically every Saturday night themselves. The timing works so they can drop me off on their way out. Now the big question is—what will I wear???

I choose my Jordache jeans. I would have killed for a pair of Gloria Vanderbilts but they aren't in my babysitting money budget. I wear a button-down shirt under a light gray crewneck sweater with light pink horizontal stripes. Preppy, but not obnoxious. This all matches my brand-new boots that I haven't even worn yet.

I saved and saved for these light gray, lace-up boots that fold over just above the ankles and the folded over part has thin, black, vertical strips. So chic. The bottoms of the boots are a little chunky for inside or outside endeavors. They are perfect, I love them, and they go so great with my light pink socks. Now my boots and socks match my sweater and they will look adorable at the movies. The movies!! With the popular girls. And I am dying to see Mr. Mom. This shapes up to be probably my best night of eighth grade so far.

Of course, I have my parents drop me off about a block from the theater. I lie and tell them I have a ride home. I'll figure that detail out later. I am to come home right after the movie, but who are they kidding? They are always out late and will never know when I come home.

I nervously walk up to the girls who are gathered in front of the theater. Did they all know I was coming? Do they really like me? What will they think of my boots and sweater combination? Well for now, my sweater is tucked away under my stylish blue winter coat. But my light pink scarf perfectly matches my socks which match the stripes on my sweater.

"Hi everyone!"

Did I squeak that out, or was it a normal voice?

"Hey Karen!"

I am welcomed in. Just like that, with a "hey." When everyone arrives, we travel like the pack of 14-year-olds we are to the front window and each buy our tickets. Once inside, we buy some snacks, and I am really struck with what to do. Do cool girls eat candy or popcorn? I hang towards the back of the pack and copy exactly what they each buy—small, buttered popcorn, regular Coke. No candy. Dang. I really love those chocolate candies with the white dots on them. Next time.

We file into a single row and take our seats. I am between Veronica on my right and Dina on my left. Dina is a big deal. We play basketball and volleyball together but never hung out before tonight. She is the youngest of like 15 kids and they live in a big house near the high school. They are all tough.

The movie is hilarious. I love it! So funny! The little guy's Woobie is so relatable to me. I still sleep with my blankie but no one, I repeat no one, knows. Plus, I stopped sucking my thumb before junior high, so I am totally grown up and cool.

After the movie, we pour out of the theater and are chatting about how funny it was. Veronica, beautiful, smart Veronica, pulls something out of her pocket. It's a round kind of box. She opens it and grabs a bunch of brown stuff and tucks it into her lower lip. She passes the box around and each of the girls grabs some and sticks it in their mouth. It's chew. They are putting chew in their mouth and it's coming my way.

Gross. No chance. But what do I do? They are so cool, and this is apparently what the cool girls do. I look down at the sidewalk as it comes my way. Just ignore it and they will pass it right by you.

"Karen! Hey, Karen! Do you want some?"

How should I answer? I want them to like me but no way. Absolutely not. My heart starts to race. I look up.

"No thanks."

"Okay, cool."

Whew. Cool. But I am getting a little nervous. Plus, I need to figure out how to get home. But then right as Veronica was working up a tobacco brown spit to shoot out of her beautiful mouth (which, by the way was covered in braces so how on earth was there not chewing tobacco in all that metal?) a group of guys walk up.

Veronica doesn't see them approaching and shoots her chew spit right onto the foot of one of the guys. He is definitely older than us—high school for sure—and he isn't happy.

At all.

"Hey, you bitch, what'd you do that for?"

Veronica giggles and tries to bat her eyelashes at him as the rest of his group walks over. They are intense. My heart starts beating so fast that I cannot hear what is being said as his group surrounds ours. All I know is that at one point Roseann grabs my hand, looks at me and says, "Vice Lords. Run!!!"

Holy crap. Vice Lords are a well-known gang from Chicago. And Veronica just spit on one of their shoes. We run west on Lake Street with our goal being to outrun these older guys. You can bet your sweet butt I am at the head of the pack.

I scream, "Where are we going?!"

"Just RUN!!!"

As we approach Harlem Avenue, I make the executive decision to turn right and head toward the Burger King. It is late and they will be open for sure. No Vice Lords will dare kill me in a Burger King on well-lit Harlem Avenue.

My arms are pumping as my new gray boots with the fold-over vertical black stripes are carrying me to safety. I have no idea what has happened to those popular girls or if they are even still alive behind me. I have the wind at my back and my perfectly feathered hair is flapping wildly.

I round into the Burger King parking lot and thank you, Jesus, there is a police car. I slow to a stop just outside the doors and the rest of the girls come slamming into me. Hands on my knees, gasping for breath, I dare turn around.

Upon seeing the squad car, those boys keep running. We are safe! Or are we? Tears sting my eyes as I face this group of girls that I want so badly to be accepted by.

"Are you kidding me? Chewing tobacco? Spitting on a Vice Lord's shoe? You guys are nuts. I need to get home."

I walk into the Burger King and walk right up to the police officers.

"Hi. My name is Karen Modder and these girls invited me to the Lake Theater to see Mr. Mom and then they started chewing tobacco and then Veronica spit her chew spit onto the shoe of what appears to be a Vice Lord and I ran all the way here and I am terrified and will someone please, please, please give me a ride home?"

And that is the first time I ride in the back of a police squad car. My parents are out with friends when I get dropped off and are none the wiser.

Country Club

My sister is in love! My parents join the country club in our town because it will be the best place to have a wedding reception. No one actually says this out loud, but I overhear Mom talking on the phone about it one day to one of her friends.

My mom, my sister, and I are excited to join because they have a big pool that has a snack bar. Dad said we have a number assigned to our family, and instead of using money, we just tell them our number and can sign for whatever food and drinks we want. What a deal!!

We are all a little nervous and excited to go to the country club pool for the first time. My sister and I are actually talking to each other about what it will be like.

"What kind of food do you think they serve? Fancy salads and stuff, or regular food like burgers? I bet the drinks taste extra good."

"I think it's all going to be fancy!"

I am wearing my brand new, bright blue Speedo swimsuit. It's got thin, white stripes that go diagonally down from my shoulder area to my hip area. Speedos are expensive and I've had my eye on this one for a while. Mom and Dad paid for most of it, and I added in some babysitting money because I wanted it so badly.

In the car, Mom, Sue, and I are all giggly and excited. We have a social membership because Mom is just starting to golf and Dad is NOT a good golfer. A social membership lets us go to the pool, eat at the restaurant, and of course—have a maybe wedding reception.

I've got my favorite rainbow beach towel around my neck and we walk through the changing rooms to the pool. My new suit is perfection as I step into the sunlight, my cool, big sis next to me. As we look for chairs, I notice a lot, well, maybe all of the girls my age are wearing green swimsuits. And not just any suit, but the exact

Speedo I am wearing in blue—except theirs are all green and they are all matching. They are also all in groups together and they all turn their heads to stare at me. There are whispers. I want to turn around and go back to the car.

"Mom?"

I turn to look up at Mom who is scanning the place for chairs.

"Mom? We need to leave."

"What? Don't be ridiculous. We just got here. Oh, look! I see three chairs together over there."

She points to an area full of green Speedos. Oh boy.

"Mom, listen to me, please."

She stops and turns to look at me.

"Mom, look at all the green suits. They are the same as mine but mine is BLUE. All of these girls match and I am the oddball. Can we please, please, please go home?"

"Oh, they must be on the swim team and that is their uniform suit. How cute! You have the same one!"

I pull my towel from around my neck and hold it in front of my new Speedo that I begged my parents to buy me and even used some of my own babysitting money on. My sister tries to make me feel better.

"Look, no one will even notice it's the same suit. Let's go swim and then get some food with our number."

I want to shrink into a tiny ball. I just know that every girl in the pool area is laughing at me. All I want is for my Speedo to magically turn into a green one. I want to match everyone else. Swim team? What the heck is a swim team? I know what it means to me. It means that all of these girls know each other and are on a team together and are probably super rich and think I'm lame for trying to be like them.

I never wear my blue Speedo there again.

Annie

Because of my lifetime love of performing, I am so excited that my high school has one of the best performing arts programs in existence! Dad signed me up for the summer musical and it is so cool because incoming freshmen can be in it. And everyone who signs up gets a part.

A few years ago, I would have thought that I'd be Annie for sure. But then in junior high, I only ever got parts in the chorus for our musicals. In 6th grade, Dad told me that I was going to be in choir starting in junior high because one of his kids was going on the big European choir trip in high school if he had anything to say about it.

Good thing I loved to sing, and Europe sounded exciting. I was all in! Ms. Simmons was our choir teacher, and she was Crabby with a capital "C." She had her favorites, and those kids always got the solos and the speaking parts in the annual musical. I was so hopeful for a part in our 8th grade musical. Can you believe Crabby Ms. Simmons chose The Puberty Blues as our musical? A bunch of kids, suffering through puberty, singing about puberty? Was she trying to torture us? I auditioned and felt good but the part I got… chorus.

Fast forward a few months and it's the first day of the summer musical. Dad drops me off in front of the main entrance to the high school and I am so excited that I jump out and head right in with my empty binder and pencil. This is a summer school class so there is some work to be done with pencils because that's all we were told to bring. A binder with a pocket, and a pencil.

Just inside the doors, there are a few steps that lead to the auditorium where the high school stage is. I take the steps in a single leap and line up to enter. There is a lady with a clipboard. I give her my name and she gives me my row and seat number. She says to go sit there right away and when all the kids are there, we will begin. I'm pretty sure everyone is as excited as I am. The seats are alphabetical, by our last names. I am so happy to see my elementary school friend Callie on one side. A skinny, and super cute guy is on the other. Callie and I chat for a minute. We sang Somewhere Over the Rainbow as part of a trio last spring at the 8th grade talent show and remind each other that we can do this. Then I turn to the guy and introduce myself.

"Hi. I'm Karen. I went to Emerson. How about you?"

"Hey, I'm Dan. I went to Hawthorne."

And that right there, was the introduction of a guy who would become one of my best friends in high school. It turns out, lockers are assigned freshman year, in alphabetical order by last name, and you keep the same locker all four years. Callie, Karen, and Dan would be next to each other for years to come.

On day one, a familiar face introduces himself as the Director. He goes to my church so I am feeling good about my chances for a part. Mr. Franklin is the Music Director. Mr. Franklin is the reason my dad got me in choir in the first place. He takes the highest choir, the A Capella Choir, to Europe for a tour every other year. My goal is to make that choir and get on that trip. I find out that it is also Dan's goal.

Auditions begin. One by one, we are to go up on the biggest stage I have ever seen, and sing the same section of Tomorrow. This is intense. So many kids are really good and sing nice and loud. Our row stands and heads to the side of the stage. Callie goes up and does a decent job. I'm up next.

I take the few steps up the side of the stage and walk out, ready to take on the musical theater world of my high school. Images of performances past flood my brain as I step into the very bright lights on the very big stage.

How did my mouth suddenly fill up with sand? Why can't I see anyone out there in the audience? Did the music just start? Oh, it did. Okay, here we go…

Suddenly, it's over and I'm thanked and walking across to the other side of the stage. What just happened? I don't remember a single thing! My mouth is thick, I feel squeaky and rubbery all at the same time. I hear Dan singing and he's doing a really good job. I don't think I've done a good job at all. I sit back down and catch my breath. Callie squeezes my hand. I don't think Ms. Simmons did such a good job of preparing us for the big-time of our high school with stupid songs about puberty. These other kids are really, really good.

Day one is all about the auditions.

Before day two begins, the cast list is posted. I search for my name at the top with the leads…no luck. Scanning lower and lower, I think I must be an orphan…no luck. I am cast as an NYC townsperson. Ugh. Callie gets orphan and she tries to make me feel better by saying I must be a townsperson because I'm too tall to be an orphan. That doesn't make me feel much better.

The days pass and groups practice onstage and in the hallways. Our school is known for putting on Broadway-like shows so it is all business, all morning, every day. If your group isn't rehearsing, you are to be studying your script and staying quiet.

Dan is outgoing and makes a lot of friends our age. They are nice guys and start a quiet little poker game on the floor, in the back of the auditorium where it is mostly dark. One day, I ask if I can play too. The guys tell me to come tomorrow and be ready to put my money where my mouth is.

"Yeah, okay, sure. I hope I don't lose all of my money to you guys!"

I show up the next morning with my LeSportSac wallet bulging. These dopes don't know that my older brother is a poker expert and taught me how to play when I was just a kid. I act dumb and surprised every time I win a hand and pull the pot towards me. Poker with the guys is fun!

"I don't know how I keep winning. You guys are great to let me play with you!"

Suddenly, through the groans of my losing cast mates, a deep voice clears as a flashlight shines onto the game from above.

"What is going on here?"

The school security guard is perched over us, and he does not seem happy.

"Oh, um, we are allowed to do quiet things when we aren't rehearsing. So we're playing some poker."

"This is gambling, and it's NOT ALLOWED on school property."

I think I'm going to faint. Security guard guy is very angry. He points the flashlight right in my face.

"You, girlie, get out of here."

I look at the guys, they are frozen. I grab my wallet and stand up slowly. Then I race back to my seat and try to breathe normally. I look back and see my poker pals getting grilled by the guard and he is writing down all of their names.

A little while later, Dan comes back to his assigned seat. He looks wiped out.

"What happened?"

"Poker for money on school property is against the law."

"What? It's just for fun."

"He said we could go to jail but we will probably all get a suspension."

"Oh my gosh. Why did he tell me to go away?"

"Yeah, you're lucky. He said we were wrong for corrupting a girl with gambling. Even though you were cleaning our clocks!"

"I am really, really sorry."

"Don't talk to me."

"But it's not fair! I was playing too!"

I stand up to go find the security guard. Dan pulls me back down.

"Listen, just leave it alone. Don't get in trouble too."

"Well, I should give you all back your money."

"No, you were better than us, just keep it. Man, my parents are going to be so mad at me."

My poker crew gets a stern talking to and some kind of mark on their high school record. Who knew playing cards for money isn't allowed? They should have it in the school handbook or something.

First Day of High School: 1984

"Karen! Get downstairs now so you can eat breakfast before school!"

Mom yells to me from the bottom of the stairwell.

"I'll be right down!"

I close my bedroom door and take one final look in the mirror. Dark jeans, yellow Polo shirt, top-siders, feathered hair sprayed into place. I smile—ugh, will these braces ever come off? I've got this. I grab my notebook and pen, and head downstairs.

"Big day today—high school!"

"I know! I'm a little nervous, Mom."

"Piece of cake. You've already done the musical. My high school years were my best years. You'll love it! I made your favorite breakfast."

"Thanks, Mom. But I think I'm too nervous to eat."

She looks disappointed so I sit. I do love Skippy's creamy peanut butter with Smucker's strawberry jelly slathered on top of a single piece of Holsum white bread. She even cut it in half, rectangle style.

"Thank you for making this. Just a couple of bites because I really think I might throw up."

"Nonsense. Roger! Time to get a move on so you can take Karen to her first big day of high school!"

My dad appears, briefcase in hand. He kisses my mom goodbye and it's time to leave. We climb into his car for the ride to school. I'm suddenly very nauseous.

"Are you ready, kiddo?"

"How close are we?"

"Just a few more blocks. You're going to love it."

My mouth is feeling dry. Maybe the peanut butter was a bad idea. I look down into my lap at my notebook. My notebook! It's yellow!! My shirt is yellow. THIS IS A CATASTROPHE.

"Dad, Dad, we've got to go back home."

"What? No, we are almost there, and I've got to catch the EL to work."

"No, no, no. We've got to go back home! My shirt is yellow, and my notebook is yellow, and they are the same yellow. Dad, everyone is going to make fun of me. We've got to go back home now so I can change my shirt."

He looks like he might be trying not to laugh. He pulls the car up, right in front of the school.

"I'm sorry Karen, but we are here. You look good. No one is going to notice."

"Dad! I cannot get out of this car. My notebook matches my shirt! Everyone will make fun of me. I can't do it. I need to go home!"

"Sorry, kiddo."

He unlocks the car and nods to my door handle.

"Time to start high school."

"Dad…"

"You've got to go."

I blink back tears, hoping they don't smudge my carefully applied blue eyeliner. My heart feels like it is going to beat right out of my chest.

"But Dad!"

He leans over me and opens the door. I have no choice. I get out of the car and turn towards my dad. He waves and pulls out into traffic. Oh boy. This is it. I turn and face the massive building that is my school now. I don't know why I am so scared when I walked in these same doors all summer. I take a deep breath as I fold the yellow cover of my notebook back and over so no one can see that it matches my shirt as I step forward and into my day. I've got this.

KAREN BROTHERS

Freshman Year Highlights

I settle into the routine of freshman year. My braces are still a dominating feature of my face, and the brown plastic frames of my glasses are in style. I decide that I love colorful, comfortable clothes and I also love The Gap. My wardrobe quickly morphs into the back wall of their store. I almost exclusively wear solid, primary-colored crewneck sweatshirts and sweatpants. It's all I ask for at Christmas and my birthday. My collection is impressive! I don't ever wear the same color top and bottom at the same time. I split them up based on my mood. Some favorite combinations include anything with red, orange, yellow, and green.

My closest friends are my friends from church. Our high school youth group is called Luther League. I'm finally old enough to hang out in the cool room in the church basement. Most of the kids from my confirmation class of nine stay connected. We meet every Sunday night and do fun things, as well as serious conversations. We take a fall and a spring retreat to a Bible camp and it is so much fun! We sleep in cabins and have chapel in the woods, play volleyball, and all kinds of games. Walking in the woods, on the guided path, at night is so much fun. The older kids are mostly nice to us freshmen and it feels good to belong to a group.

I'm still friends with some junior high kids, but after the Mr. Mom debacle, I'm cautious. The freshman girls' choir is fun. After being a lousy townsperson in Annie, I'm too nervous to audition for the big musical but I take an acting class as an elective. I love performing and especially making people laugh. Our high school theater program turns out legit, real-life stars, and I worry about having what it takes. I find out that while I was self-producing, directing, and starring in shows in the 'hood, other kids were signing up for real theater classes and shows. I thought I knew what I was doing, but they really did.

My older brother and sister are both off at the same college. It can be lonely at home sometimes. I've made my sister's room into my make-up and hair styling room, and my brother's room is my TV lounge. I mostly stay in my own room, but I really like the idea of spreading out into theirs. They do NOT know that I've got some of my stuff in both of their rooms. It's kind of cool though because when I miss them, it's nice to hang out in their space.

At the end of freshman year, there are all kinds of things to choose from for teams. I've played softball for most of my life and it's probably my best sport, but I want to try something new. Field hockey is something I've never played, and I go to the after-school workshops leading up to the tryouts. The last day of field hockey workshops is also the first day of cheerleading workshops. That sounds really fun, and I've never done that either. I decide to switch it up and try out for cheerleading instead.

I haven't done much tumbling since I was younger, and the cheerleaders need a few skills. Every night, after the workshops, I head to the basement where we still have the gymnastics mat. I perfect my round-off but nothing else seems to be coming back to me. I hope the round-off is enough.

And I make it! I am going to be part of the sophomore cheer squad. A cheerleader!! Mom is so stoked that I'll be a cheerleader. She was never a cheerleader, and she thinks it is a good thing to be. Wow does it feel good to make something! We have an after-school meeting and the girls seem really nice. We will start practices over the summer and even go to camp together. This is better than I could have imagined!

I also try out for the Orchesis dance team. That seems to be the coolest kids in the whole school. It didn't matter that I hadn't taken a single dance class since I was five, I was flexible and loved to dance. Surely, I'd make the team. I did not. I was told I'd never make it as long as I wore glasses.

I go and get contact lenses and vow to try again next year. I will take every dance class in P.E. and maybe even the summer dance classes for summer school. I know I can do it!

Sophomore Year: 1985-86

Some of my friends from church don't like that I'm a cheerleader. There's an older girl in our group of friends and I think she told the girls my age that now that I'm a cheerleader I'm going to be different. I'm still the same me and that makes me sad. But I'm determined to make my mark in high school. I love meeting new people and getting involved in things.

I also am elected to Student Council and get to represent my class! We are in charge of everything to do with Homecoming and I like being on all of the committees. Now, if I could only get a date to the dance.

I get a super short, pixie style haircut (who knew voluminous hair was about to be all the rage?) and trade in my brown glasses for a pair of light blue. My quest to find a date to Homecoming is on track.

Guess what I learn? You can ride a float in the Homecoming parade, cheer at the game, and if you are on Student Council and don't have a date, well, then you still have to work getting everything ready for the dance that you aren't attending.

My 16th birthday is in March, and I cannot wait to get my driver's license. For my birthday, I ask for a shopping spree at Marshall Field's on State Street in Chicago. Mom and I spend a whole day and I get three new outfits, mostly ESPRIT. They are so cute! I get a black, stretch pencil skirt with a short-sleeved button-down shirt with a funky pattern of like city people and stuff. Then a matching cool, kind of dark coral cardigan sweater that goes over it. The other outfits are mostly the same and so funky and cool. I get them in green and black and purple and black. The pants are leggings with thin, horizontal stripes. The tops are big sweaters with shoulder pads that have really thick horizontal stripes. I love it all so much!

Then for my friend party, Mom lets me have an actual dinner party at the dining room table. All of my friends come, and it is fun to have different friends from different groups. Mom makes my favorite—sloppy joe's, orange jello with mandarin orange slices, and the incredible chocolate éclair dessert. Everyone wears the same Erin Go Braugh hats I've had at every birthday party for as long as I can remember. It is so much fun, and I feel so lucky!

Then comes my family party. I wear the black skirt, printed shirt, cardigan combo. Mom and Dad have another big gift for me. Wow! They already spent so much money on my clothes from Chicago, I can't imagine what it could be. Our family parties are always so fun and this one is no different. When it comes time to open gifts, Mom sits right next to me. I have to open their present first and she is so excited. It is big, but not too heavy.

I slowly peel back the tape on one corner, teasing her in front of everyone because she is so excited. Then I laugh and just rip the paper right off, revealing…Cabbage Patch Twin dolls. My mom squeals in delight. I am literally stunned. Dolls? I'm sixteen. I have friends getting cars as gifts and I get…dolls? My aunt quickly hands her gift to me. She is as excited as my mom. My thoughtful aunt hand sewed a bunch of matching outfits…for my new dolls. Wow.

Wow. I fake a smile and all of my cousins are trying not to laugh. It's hard being the second youngest! But Mom is so excited, so I just roll with it and smile for the pictures. I'm secretly so glad that we went shopping and I got all of the cool clothes. My parents might not think of me as growing up, but it's happening whether they like it or not.

Sophomore year is a year of making new friends and establishing my high school self. As the school year ends, I decide to up my game. I leave cheer (Well, I didn't make Varsity. Apparently, a clean round-off doesn't cut it in the big leagues), join the JV Drill Team, finally make the Orchesis Dance Team, try out for the synchronized swim team and do NOT make it, but I do win an election to be Junior Class President. I fully run for class office because the Junior Class plans the Junior/Senior Prom. This is the sole and only reason I run—I think I'm good at planning things!

After preparing since junior high choir, I audition for, and make our school's highest choir—A Capella! I am in the chorus for another summer musical and make even more new friends.

Summer of 1986

This summer is going to be so exciting. Mom and Dad hired a private voice coach all last semester. During study halls, I met with her with one goal in mind: to learn, perfect, and then sing The Wedding Song at my sister's wedding in June. In my four years of singing in a choir, I've never gotten a solo, but that doesn't matter because Mom thinks I've got what it takes and I know I can do it. Even though I've only been in an official choir for four years, I have been a performer since I could pretty much walk. I'm nervous, but I know I can do it. I'm an alto, and my voice teacher told me that might work against me. For our end-of-the-year voice recital, my piece is Swing Low, Sweet Chariot. I waver a bit, but nail it in the end. June 21—I'm ready for you!

My hair is growing out and I am excited to achieve some of the big hair looks that are becoming popular. The week before the wedding, Mom convinces me to cut my hair short again.

"Oh, Mom, I don't know. I think really big hair is in style."

"No, you look so nice with a good short cut."

"But I've been growing it out."

"And it's in the funny, in-between stage. It will look darling short."

So, I get my hair cut short with layers in the front so I can feather it. It's a lot of work to achieve the perfect feather and my hair just wants to lay flat on my head. I buy all of the curling iron sizes with my own money and practice and practice for the big wedding day.

A few weeks before the wedding, Mom calls me down from my room.

"Karen! Come downstairs!"

I carefully put my curling iron down on my vanity, making sure it's clear of anything it might light on fire.

"Coming!"

Mom is sitting at her little desk with important lists in front of her.

"Karen, we have hired a professional singer to sing at your sister's wedding. Now you don't have to worry about that and can just have fun. Isn't that great?"

"What? But I have been working so hard on the song. You paid a voice teacher. I memorized all of the words."

"It's for the best. That's all."

She checked off something on her list. It was me. She checked me right off the list. I stand up and walk right out the back door before she can see the tears rolling down my face.

It's cloudy outside and smells like it might rain. I don't care. I walk down the steps, through the yard, and into the shortcut. I lean against the Tanner's garage and will the tears to stop coming.

Listen, she's right, you aren't a soloist. It will be better this way. You'll have more fun.

I remember my curling iron is plugged in up in my room and wipe off my face. I take my fists and push them into my eyeballs.

Stop it. Stop crying. You're not a soloist. It will be better this way. You'll have more fun.

Deep breath as I head back into the yard, up the stairs, and into the kitchen. Mom is still at the table.

"You're right Mom, I'm not a soloist. It will be better this way. I'll have more fun."

I walk up to my room and sit down at my vanity. I turn off my curling iron and stare at myself in my Hollywood lights make-up mirror. I turn off the lights and keep staring.

Your hair is dumb. Singing is dumb. This wedding is dumb.

The Rehearsal Dinner

My sister's wedding is tomorrow. We just finished the practicing at the church stuff and now we are heading to Chicago on a fancy bus that my future brother-in-law's parents rented for all of us to drive in. The seats are plush and there is even a bathroom in here!

"Mom? Where is the dinner?"

"In Chicago, at a very exclusive restaurant. We are so lucky!"

"Where is it though?"

For some reason I am a little nervous.

"You'll see soon enough!"

Everyone is in a great mood. Sue and Pete are so in love and I'm excited to be a bridesmaid for the first time ever. The movie Sixteen Candles is one of my all-time favorites and I hope my Jake Ryan shows up. Of course, I don't know who he is, but any hot guy will do. Any hot guy that notices me would be just great. A glance my way even…

Enough dreaming! We are in the city and the bus is pulling up to a building and it's time to get out. Once on the sidewalk, I look up. It's the John Hancock Building.

"Mom, is there a restaurant in here?"

"Yes."

We all walk into the lobby and head towards the elevators. My sister holds my hand.

"Where is the restaurant?"

My heart is racing, and my mouth feels full of cotton.

"It's up on the 95th floor."

The doors open and she gently pulls me in with the crowd.

"What? But I am so afraid of heights. I can't go up there."

The elevator climbs and I squeeze Sue's hand tighter. She doesn't let go. I look through the people over towards Mom and she is giving me that "don't-you-dare-ruin-this" look. The elevator keeps going up. Sue looks at me.

"It will be fine. You will be okay. It's a fun night of celebrating. You can do it."

The elevator doors open, revealing large windows in front of me. I instinctively let out a blood-curdling scream and drop flat on my stomach, never letting go of my sister's hand. People are stepping around me. Dad has both of his hands on top of his head. Mom is giving me death glares. I'm pretty sure my brother and Pete's brothers are laughing at me. I don't know what to do. I am ruining my sister's special night. I know that for a fact.

She squats next to me.

"I won't let go of your hand. It's going to be okay. Get up right now."

I don't want to get up. I am so scared that I will fall right out of the windows. I'm even more afraid that if there is an open window, I will jump. That doesn't even make any sense but that is what I am feeling.

"I am so scared. I can't get up, but I don't want to ruin your night."

"Get up right now."

I stand up, gripping my sister. Everyone that turned to stare at me when I screamed seems to be minding their own business again. My mom walks up to me with a glass of wine.

"Drink this right now. It will calm you down."

I pretend like I've never had alcohol before.

"Mom, this is illegal."

She puts the glass to my lips and starts to tilt it up. I take it from her because I don't want it to spill on my special dress for the night. I drink it down and hand her back the glass. I am still holding my sister's hand. We slowly walk to the special room Pete's parents have reserved for us. It is a special night, and I am sure that it cost so much money and I am ruining it all. I don't mean to. I am trying not to cry as we walk.

I whisper to my sister, "I'm sorry."

"It's okay. But lighten up on your grip a little. I can't feel my hand."

We get to the room. It is long and narrow. One whole side is windows that I think take up the whole wall. There is one long table and there are assigned seats. Pete's mom comes up and points to where my seat is at the end of the table.

"Um, I'm sorry, but I don't think I can let go of my sister's hand."

Mom comes up.

"Karen, this is a beautiful night, and your seat is down there. You must let go and go to your seat."

I am terrified. I am frozen in place. I can only look at the floor or the ceiling. I cannot look out those windows. Everything is feeling blurry because my tears are hot and filling up my eyes.

"I can't let go."

My sister says it's fine, I can just sit next to her. That was where her Maid of Honor was supposed to sit and I know, I just know, that I am ruining everything. I want to go home and crawl into my bed. But this is an important night and I've got to hang in there. My mom brings me another glass of wine. Pete's mom does not at all like that she is giving a sixteen-year-old girl alcohol, but Mom tells her she needs to do something to calm me down.

Mom is disappointed. Dad is fed up. Sue is being nice, but I just want to melt away.

At some point, I am able to let go of her. Then someone stands up and leans against the window wall to take a picture with their camera. I can't help it. I scream again. I am so off balance, and I am so tired. I try my best to be a good sister, a good bridesmaid, a good daughter. I try but I don't think I'm doing a good job.

The Wedding

I survived the rehearsal dinner, and the wedding is finally here. I can't get my hair to feather the right way, so Mom lets me get it done at the hair salon. The girl mostly uses a round brush, blow dryer, and a bunch of hair spray. It's nothing special and I sure could have done a lot more with my collection of curling irons.

I feel kind of pretty but it's my sister's day and she looks absolutely beautiful. Mom has a gorgeous beaded pink dress, and she is loving every part of this day. When it's time to walk down the aisle, I hold the bouquet of flowers tightly and head down the long aisle of our church. Step together, step together. My face is hurting because I'm smiling so much. I'm so glad I got my braces off, and my pearly whites are on full display.

After the wedding, the reception is at the country club. Which, by the way, I never did make a single friend at the pool. Not one single friend. But the room is nice and it is fancy so Mom is happy. The party is a blast and my brother and Pete's brother bring me screwdrivers to drink all night. Yum! It's great because everyone thinks I am just drinking orange juice, but it's really got vodka in it. Ha!

Once the reception is over, my parents have their friends over at our house for an after-party. My parents always host the best parties. I have had a lot of orange juice and vodka at this point, and I am tired. I decide to just lay down on the living room floor. The shag carpet is so soft and comfy…

This is where I wake up the next morning—face down on the floor, carpet smooshed into my face, pink bridesmaid dress and all.

Fall 1987

Sue's wedding is behind us and it is time for me to really make my mark—junior year of high school! I have worked hard to secure spots in all of the things that I think are important. I have friends in all of the groups. I'm trying to find my best friend and I think it might be between Amanda and Jenny. We were all on sophomore cheer together and now we are on JV Drill Team. They are the sweetest and we have a lot of fun.

Amanda and I really cemented our bond on cheer. After Drill Team practice on most days, we walk over to Tasty Dog and get cheese fries and a pop. Then we walk home together up Fair Oaks Ave. She lives off Fair Oaks and down to the right a few blocks before I turn off. So we talk about all kinds of things on our walks. She is a really good listener!

Jenny is funny and we have so many laughs. We are starting to do a lot of sleepovers. Her parents are so nice, and their house is really cool. They have a family room that's down a few stairs, kind of sunken. Outside of a sliding glass door (how cool!) they have a hot tub! Screwdrivers are now my drink of choice and Jenny's parents don't drink. We mix them up and sit in the hot tub when I sleep over. We feel very grown up and boy, do we laugh a lot!

I put a lot of time and energy into planning Homecoming and there is no way I'm going to miss it! There seem to be zero guys interested in asking me, so Jenny sets me up with her boyfriend's friend. He is nice and he is funny. This could be fun. And maybe, just maybe, I might get my first kiss at some point!

Well, he agrees to be my date but only if I will pay for the ticket, the dinner, and the limo. He says he will pay my dad back for his share of the limo but I am not holding my breath on that one.

The night of the dance comes and I am wearing the dress I wore to my sister's rehearsal dinner. My hair is still shorter than I want but I am growing it out so I pin it back, half-up half-down, with a pretty barrette and curl my bangs and the rest of it under. I've been practicing wearing my eyeliner under my eye, not just on the rim of the lower lid. Not bad.

The dance is fun! Student Council did a good job with all of the decorations. My date is nowhere to be found for the entire dance, but he does surface when it's time to leave. Our group heads out for dinner and now the limo is dropping each of us off. I'm first.

Please, God, if you're there, let my date get out of the car with me and even though I'm not sure if he knows my name, let him do the right thing and kiss me goodnight. Please, God. I am begging you for this.

The limo glides to a stop in front of my house. I look at Jenny and she nods. I smile shyly and look at my date. He is staring right at me. He nods towards the door. Jenny nods towards him. I open the door and step out. Could this be it??? Might I get a first kiss?

He steps out behind me. I do a gentle pivot on my patent leather ballet flat and turn to face him, eyes hopeful, looking up through my glasses. He looks right into my soul and speaks…

"Well, yeah, um, bye!"

He gets back in the limo and it drives away leaving me standing, unkissed on my front lawn. Ugh! I am so angry!! He basically ditched me at the dance, hardly said a word at dinner, forgot to pay me for the limo, and then didn't even kiss me goodnight. UGH!

I go inside where my mom is pacing in the darkened front room, lit cigarette leading the way. She must have seen everything.

"How was the dance?"

"It was fine."

"Nice young man."

"I guess."

"Don't worry, you'll find a boyfriend."

"I guess. Good night, Mom."

I walk up to my room, grab my Kodak Disk camera, and snap a picture of myself. I never want to forget how bad I feel right now.

What did Mom mean by that? "Don't worry, you'll find a boyfriend?" She always, always had a boyfriend in high school. That's all she talks about when she does share anything about when she was a teenager. Then Sue always, always had a boyfriend. What is wrong with me? I can't even get a date to Homecoming without bribing someone to go with me. I can't even get a boy to kiss me. I'm the worst.

MOXIE MATTERS

January 4, 1987

King of Hearts. The turnabout dance that I can go to. Well…I can go if I can find a date willing to go with me. But I've got a plan and tonight when I get home from Aunt Carole and Uncle Ron's house, I will put it in action. I love celebrating Christmas with them and boy do they spoil me! I love that Aunt Carole and Mom have been friends their whole lives and that she is my godmother is such a bonus!

The car ride home is only 45 minutes but it feels like an eternity. I've got to get home to call Pat Brady and ask him to King of Hearts. I can't believe I waited this long to call him and ask. I am such a dork. We've been friends since sophomore year and all of our other friends are going together. It makes so much sense that we should go. It is going to be so much fun. Our group will be Melanie and Dan, Jenny and Doug, Kim and Norm. Agh! I can't wait.

"Mom! Please, please don't smoke in the car. Ugh!"

"Listen, it's not going to hurt you. Let me have some peace."

"But my hair and my clothes are going to smell SO BAD!"

"Enough!"

"Dad, when will we be home? Are we almost home?"

"Karen, calm yourself. We've got about fifteen minutes. You have a date or something?"

My parents both started laughing at that.

"No. I don't have a date. But I have something really important to do. Why are you guys laughing at me? Is it so hard to think I might actually have a date?"

"Oh Karen, calm down. I only hope you'll find a boyfriend soon. Your sister had a couple of boyfriends by her junior year."

"Yeah, Mom, I know okay? Geez."

I sink down into my seat and try not to inhale the putrid smell of my mom's Benson & Hedges. It's so disgusting and now I'm going to have to wash my hair before school tomorrow because it wreaks. I open the back window for some fresh air.

"Karen Melissa! Close that window right now, it's freezing outside!"

This blows. I can't get home fast enough. The smoke clears. I am close to being lulled to sleep in the back seat of Dad's Oldsmobile if it wasn't for one thing—as soon as we get home, I am going to head right upstairs, grab the hallway phone, and pull that curly cord until it safely reaches my bedroom. I will call Pat Brady and ask him to the dance.

"Hi, is Pat there?"

"Just a minute. Paaaaat! Phone call!"

"Yeah?" Pat would pick up the phone.

"Pat? Hi, it's Karen Modder."

"Oh, hi! I was hoping it was you."

"Well great! I wanted to ask you to be my date for King of Hearts."

"Excellent! Yes, yes, I would love to be your date. I'm so glad you called…"

As we pull into our driveway, my hand is on the door handle. I am ready to go and execute my Karen-gets-a-date-to-the-dance mission. The car stops, I lean forward, and Dad turns to me.

"Karen. Stay put."

"Wait, why is Mom getting out of the car? Mom?"

The door shuts and she walks up the driveway.

"We're going to drive over to Sue and Pete's. There's something we need to discuss."

"What?! We were just with them. What is happening Dad? I've got something really, really important to do!"

"Just calm yourself. We've got to go to Sue and Pete's to talk to them about something that is actually important."

He is nervous as he answers me. Why is he nervous? I'M NERVOUS because I've got to get inside and make that call. Word on the street is that someone else is going to ask Pat Brady to King of Hearts too. I have to get to him first.

"But why doesn't Mom have to go? Dad!"

"Calm yourself."

I sink into my seat and fume. Hot tears of anger spring to my eyes. I just know someone else will get to Pat first and I'll miss my only chance to go to this dance. Life is so unfair! I hate my parents for making me miss this phone call.

We ride the ten minutes to my sister's apartment in silence. What do we have to talk about that we couldn't have talked about earlier today? Why are we doing this? Why isn't Mom coming with? It's such bullshit. Oh wait. Are we in trouble for something? Sue and I have been fighting a lot lately but come on, we're sisters!

"Dad. What do we have to talk about? Are we in trouble?"

"Karen, we're here. Let's go up to their apartment and then we can talk."

"Ugh!"

I stomp my feet as we walk up to Sue and Pete's apartment. The other girl likely has already gotten to Pat. Now what will I do? I know what. I stomp my feet even harder as we climb the stairs to their place.

"Dad, can we make this fast? I've got something that is actually truly important to do tonight."

Sue and Pete look surprised to see us and we all sit down. I take the couch with my new brother-in-law, Sue's in her rocking chair, and Dad pulls up a kitchen chair. Let's go.

Dad tells us all to sit down. Then he looks at the floor.

He is barely whispering. "Your mom, um, your mom has cancer."

The room freezes. A hard buzzing sound fills my entire head. I go numb.

What did he just say?

He continues on.

"She has cancer in her…in her…breast. Breast cancer."

I can't speak. I can't move. I stop breathing.

What did he just say?

"She's been sick for over a year. With cancer."

A year?

"Why didn't you tell us sooner?"

Someone manages to ask. Was it me?

"Well Susan was getting married, and we didn't want the news to ruin the wedding. Then it was Christmas, and we didn't want to ruin Christmas so…"

So…you chose tonight and ruined my chances of going to yet another dance???

Did I say that out loud? No, no, it doesn't seem like I said that out loud. But what did he just say?

"She's already had some procedures."

"Procedures? Like surgeries?" This is, in fact, me talking.

"Yes. Those weekend trips we took. Well, she was really in the hospital."

"So, you waited all this time to tell us. Why are you telling us now?"

"She is going to start chemotherapy. It is time to tell you."

It is time to tell us? Mom has cancer? She's already had "procedures"? Chemotherapy?

"Why isn't Mom here now?"

"It is too hard for her."

Ah.

"Oh, and a couple of people know but she doesn't want anyone else to know just yet. We don't want you to tell anyone."

Wait. What did he just say?

I don't remember walking back down the flights of stairs that I had just stomped up minutes ago. But we are in the car, driving home. I am mute. My mind reels. I feel sick.

My mom has cancer and is going to have chemotherapy. She has already had procedures and my parents lied to us for over a year. Only a few people know, and I am not supposed to tell anyone. These thoughts play over and over in my head.

When we get home, Mom is in bed. Dad tells me to leave her be, this was a hard night for her.

I go to my bedroom and bury my face in my pillow. Tears pour out of me in violent, silent, screaming sobs. I am terrified. I was supposed to ask Pat Brady to King of Hearts tonight. I wasn't supposed to find out my mom has cancer.

January 5, 1987

The very next morning, my friends gather in our usual spot at the lockers before class. My mind is still spinning with the information Dad shared last night.

Mom has cancer. She's going to have chemotherapy. She's had it for over a year. Don't tell anyone.

The big news of the hallway is that another girl did ask Pat to the dance.

"Karen! What happened?"

"Why didn't you ask him?"

"Ugh, our group is going to suck now! Why didn't you call him?"

"Karen? Karen!"

"Hmmm? I, um, I just didn't."

My head literally buzzes, and I feel like I am walking through the thickest fog with everything around me slowly being muted as I walk to my first period class, Student Council. Our faculty leader, Mr. Magel, starts our daily meeting. I feel detached from my body. I am dizzy and think I am going to throw up.

Mom has cancer. She's going to have chemotherapy. She's had it for over a year. Don't tell anyone.

I stand up and walk to the bathroom. It is down the hall a bit and around a corner. Tears start filling my eyes as I walk, then start to run. I can't breathe. When I get to the bathroom, I slide down a wall and sit with tears streaming down my face. I gulp air into my lungs. Have I actually stopped breathing?

A friend shows up a few minutes later.

She bends down, "Karen? What's happening? Are you okay?"

Big inhale. Where was all the air?

"Um no. No, I'm not okay."

I look up and her face is blurry, so I look past her and tell the wall, "My mom has cancer. I'm not supposed to tell anyone."

Then the tears come like a waterfall. Tears and snot and anger and confusion all pour right out of me.

She ran right out of the bathroom. Great, I scared her away and now I'm totally alone.

But, not for long. She hustled back to our classroom. She gathered an army of friends who all come into the bathroom to comfort and support me. Guys, girls, perhaps the entire Student Council. Some sit with me on the ground, some stand. But they are with me.

I am not sitting alone.

I'm Trying

Life at home is difficult. When my older brother and sister were in high school, their lives were very different than mine. My sister seemed to float from one serious boyfriend to the next and Mom loved it because it reminded her of all her high school boyfriends. Which then layers the pressure on me to get a boyfriend. "Why don't you have a boyfriend?" is a common question I am asked. My response? "I'm trying."

My brother's high school experience was good grades, baseball, and Atari. He hardly ever had any chores that I ever saw. I really look up to him, so it never bothered me.

Now my brother is away at college and my sister is married and living her perfect life. It doesn't seem fair to me, and my resentment grows.

We grew up with our mom as a stereotypical homemaker and stay-at-home mom. My siblings learned how to do laundry the night before they left for college. They only cooked when a cooking class assigned a project at home.

I am now being expected to do the family laundry, pick up around the house, and make occasional meals. I don't mind though because I want to help. I want to be seen as trying to make things better.

No one ever explains Mom's illness to me in any way. Sue and Pete come over sometimes, but I am not included in any discussions. I guess I could wander in and sit down, but I get the distinct impression that I am not wanted. Maybe they are trying to protect me, but I am old enough to understand.

I only know these facts: she has cancer, is getting chemo, and we have to keep things quiet for a variety of reasons. Her own parents can't know because my grandmother is convinced she herself has cancer and talks about it non-stop. She is healthy for a grandma.

My mom doesn't want people at church to know she is sick because she doesn't want them bringing us meals. I want them bringing us meals.

I understand the secrecy at times because I think my parents are coming to terms with what is happening. And then I thought they'd gradually let more people in. Which, they are, but it is slow and the people who know are very few. I don't know who knows and who doesn't. All our neighbors who feel like bonus parents to me are no longer a safe place for me to land because I don't know if they know. Why can't people know?

As a result, my friends become even more important to me. Their homes are my sanctuary. Before Mom got cancer, I was really involved in Luther League. But now she doesn't want church people to know so I pull away. I really miss those friends and the weekly activities that are not only fun but do actually make me want to know more about God.

I feel all twisted and turned around. Nighttime phone calls with my friends become a lifeline of sorts.

If someone in our family needs the phone, they just pick up a receiver and tell whomever is on the phone to get off. I get tired of walking on eggshells at home and balancing secrets. I am in my room, lamenting on the phone with a friend.

"It's all so unfair. I've got to keep up with my schoolwork, my teams, government, all of it! I don't understand why it's all such a big secret and my mom is being the biggest bitch."

Then I hear the sound that I never want to hear—a soft click. Someone is on the line downstairs and heard me. What did they hear? I know quickly when I hear the screaming. My heart sinks and the bile rises in my throat.

"Oh no. My mom was just on the line. She heard me. Oh no. I've got to go." I whisper a good-bye to my friend.

I push the heels of my hands into my eye sockets to will my eyes not to cry. Why was she listening? Don't I have any privacy?

What is wrong with her?! I am angry and also terrified. We aren't allowed to say fart or even poo in my house. Bitch is way up there on the list of horrible things to be punished for saying.

Rolling off my inflatable mattress lounge zone, I stand up and open my bedroom door. As I walk slowly down the stairs my heart sinks with each step I take. I can hear Mom crying. She is sobbing. This isn't good. Beyond the punishment I know is coming, I think I hurt her feelings. If only it was that simple.

Dad turns quickly, fuming, when I appear at the bottom of the stairs.

"Look at what you've done!" He screams as he points towards my mom.

She is sitting in her usual kitchen chair at her little desk area on the side of the table. Both of her hands are on her heart, and she is crying and very pale.

I can't speak. I can barely look at my dad.

"Do you know what you've done?!" he continues. "The chemo makes her heart weak! Your filthy words upset her so much that she might be having a heart attack right now!"

With these words, he starts running around the kitchen gathering things.

Mom just looks at me, trying to breathe, tears running down her face.

I am absolutely terrified. I try to help get her up but am told to stay away from her because I have done enough damage. Following them to the front door, I have no words.

They leave for the emergency room. How am I supposed to know she is ripe for a heart attack because of the chemo? No one tells me anything at all about her illness. I know she still has her hair because she wears some cooling contraption on her head during the treatments. I noticed she is quieter and more withdrawn but is still living her life. So I thought I was supposed to go ahead and live my life too.

It is all so unfair.

It is all so scary.

I am just a typical teenage girl, complaining about my mom on the phone with my friend, and it appears that she might now die because of my words.

She comes home from the ER that night and after Dad tucks her into their bed, I go down and crawl in next to her.

"I'm so sorry Mommy. I didn't mean it. I was just upset. I don't want to ever hurt you. I want to help. I'm so sorry, Mommy. I love you."

I stay there until she falls asleep.

Days pass and she continues to get weaker and sicker. There is still no real explanation to me. I help around the house doing laundry and making meals. I also recommit my efforts to finding a boyfriend and making her proud of everything I am doing.

Spring, 1987

As junior year of high school progresses my fashion sense improves. I am now adorned with shoulder pads on top of shoulder pads, my short hair is finally growing out and my contacts win out over my glasses. Surely these will be the deciding factor in reaching my new goal to have actually and finally a real, first kiss.

I am seventeen years old and un-kissed. This has to change. It becomes a mission of sorts for my group of friends. I am both thankful and mortified. One Friday night, at a random house party, a guy I'm going to call "Spits" is recruited for the job. He secures the keys to a friend's dad's Cadillac and walks up to me.

"Hey Modder. Let's go for a ride."

"Yeah, okay, let's go."

It is time.

"Where are we headed?"

"To my favorite place in town."

He is a nice enough guy. Off we drive to our destination—the rooftop of the centrally located parking garage in town. Romantic! Within seconds of parking, he hits the power seat button. Whoa, I'm on the move. I am horizontal when he flips right on top of me. Time for my magical first kiss!

It happens so fast; my head is spinning. I don't really mind his body on top of mine, he's kind of thin. I look at his face and see his open mouth as it slams down onto mine. It is like a waterfall of saliva, and it comes crashing down on my face. His lips are kind of sliding all around mine and spit is dripping down my chin.

Not what I expected, but I am being kissed so I go with it.

I don't know if seconds, or minutes, pass, but I dare to open my eyes as we take a break and Spits hovers a good eight inches above my face. We are still connected by thick strands of spit pouring from all around his mouth to mine. I'm kind of gurgling through it all and not sure what I'm supposed to do.

Thankfully, we break soon, and I towel off. (Not really, but wow, a towel would have been helpful.) I use both hands to wipe all the excess slobber from my face and onto my leggings.

He flops back to his seat and raises mine. What a fancy car! I look over at him.

"So, yeah…"

I don't know if we're going out now or what.

"No big deal. Happy to help."

I am totally embarrassed but honestly, I get over it pretty fast. I've been kissed. It's done. We drive back to the party, and I am so happy.

I've been kissed. I've been kissed. I've been kissed!!!

I am not sure how much I liked it, but it was done. Spits is a good guy who rose to the challenge and provided me with a splashy experience.

The very next night, I go to a small party at a friend's house. I am delighted to see a cutie who has just moved to our town from Iowa. His nickname is "Corn." Every girl I know is interested in him. I am feeling rather confident in myself because I have now been kissed. I sit down next to Corn on a couch.

"Hey Corn, what's up?"

"Not much."

I'm not quite sure how it happened, but Corn and I are suddenly under a blanket, in the middle of the party. I go for it. He responds.

I have now kissed my second boy and it was SO MUCH BETTER. I wasn't slathered in saliva. Corn knows what he is doing. Now maybe I will too. Sorry Spits.

My friends are thrilled for me, and I am welcomed to the cafeteria table the following Monday to applause and cheers.

First kiss, check. Second kiss, even better, check.

Junior Prom

As Junior Class President, one of my responsibilities is to plan the 1987 Junior/Senior Prom. I am crazy hopeful to get a date for the prom that I am planning for 800+ of my classmates. Finding a date has never been easy and it genuinely brings me great sadness. I feel a lot of pressure from home to not only secure dates to dances, but to get an actual boyfriend.

Good news—I got a date!

As the head of the prom committee, I have worked so hard. Leading and planning come easily to me. Together with my team, I secured a fancy hotel in the heart of downtown Chicago. I personally chose the menu and supervised the decorations.

The big day is here. All of the planning is done and I am ready to have fun with my friends.

My dress is everything a prom dress in 1987 should be. It has a pink satin strapless bodice with a larger-than-life sequin bow sewn right across my less-than-ample chest. The bottom half is tea length with layers of lace upon even more layers of tulle. I got not only my shoes, but my purse dyed to match at Baker's Shoes at the mall. Contacts in, hair the appropriate volume for the times—I am a vision in my own eyes.

Mom is home from another short stay at the hospital and able to see me off and be part of the pictures with my date and some friends. She is leaning against the wall of the doorway to the front room, watching with a big grin, and I know she is happy her youngest daughter has an actual date.

I hope she is proud of all the planning that I have done to make it an incredible night for my classmates. Mom and I don't communicate much at this point. Everyone in our family is just moving forward each day, doing their own thing. My sister, the newlywed; my brother away at college; and I am pouring myself into high school activities and friends. I miss the connection with my family, and especially my mom. Sadly, I didn't know how to say that and maybe even more sadly, no one is asking.

Ever since Mom's breast cancer diagnosis, the family feels like we are shutting down. My parents seem very secretive about treatments, and I crave information so I can know what is happening. Keeping busy seems to help push my fear away.

After months of preparation, getting a date, and scoring the perfect dress, I am so glad this night is finally here: my junior prom. After pictures of our group flanking the fake fireplace in our front room, our small group leaves for that dance full of hope for memories to be made.

Chaperones, who are all teachers, are welcoming students at the doors to the ballroom. Anyone suspicious looking is flagged and assessed for level of intoxication. A few kids are leaning heavily against the wall. This makes no sense to me. Why get drunk before the dance? The magical dance where any sort of wonderful thing could happen?

We make it through and when I walk into the ballroom, it takes my breath away. The high ceilings, huge crystal chandeliers, and so many people. I am nervous for everything to go well. I feel the weight of the success of this night directly on my shoulders and that is feeling extra weighty in my adorable strapless dress.

Finding our table, Jenny and I weave our way through the throngs of seniors, who all look like full-fledged adults in my eyes. They look us up and down, I'm sure checking to see if our shoes are adequately dyed. I get the definite feeling these seniors do not approve of us juniors crashing their party. But don't they know I planned it for them? Don't they know how much work I put in? It doesn't matter. I am standing in the middle of the best party of my life and I am going to enjoy it all.

Dinner is served and the energy levels are high. The band begins to play, and everyone swarms to the dance floor. The music is pumping and the room is vibrating from both the excitement of the night and the bass from the band. Billy Idol is the BEST. I'm so glad the band is playing this. Everyone is going nuts! Oh my gosh, I think it's safe to say this night is a success. Just look at everyone, all decked out. Jenny calls out to me.

"Karen get out here!! Dance! Have fun!"

"Okay, okay! I was having so much fun just watching everyone! I'm coming!"

I run as fast as my two-inch, Baker's-dyed pumps can take me, and we push our way to our other friends. It's hard to move through because everyone is literally smashed up against each other and jumping up and down.

I let go, throw my hands in the air, and get carried away into the iconic Billy Idol song.

"Karen you did it!"

"What an awesome night!"

We all start screaming, "Hey mother..." and then silence. Everyone keeps chanting but I stop mid-jump and look to the side of the stage. The hotel event manager, my contact, is standing there holding a huge cord. The energy in the room is totally gone as everyone stops and turns to stare at the band on the stage. The band is angry and confused as the event manager starts shouting my name. Ugh! What is happening??

I leave Jenny and head for the stage. I start pushing my way through my peers.

Everyone is covered in sweat. Bow ties are on top of foreheads, shirts are clinging to skin, and amazingly most every girl's hair is still perfectly in place. AquaNet for the win!

I keep making my way to the side of the stage. All of the seniors are up at the front and whoa, there's the Senior Class President, a neighbor and kid I've known growing up. He looks right at me and opens his eyes super wide. My mouth goes dry as I shrug. I have no idea what's happening, but this is my event and I'm the name being screamed into mass of sweaty teens.

As I get closer to the event manager, I notice he's got someone standing next to him. What the heck? Who is that? Why are they wearing that hideous shirt? Wait, is that a cane? My heart starts racing as every junior and senior prom goer from my high school starts chanting, "Music, music, music, music!" This can't be good.

I finally squeeze my way through the senior Drill Team girls who happily give me a little shove to get through the last bit of senior judgment wrapped in taffeta and tulle.

"Karen, this is Stan. He's the Chairman of the Midwest Blind Bowlers Association. Their event is happening downstairs right now and all of you kids are completely disorienting them with your jumping! THE JUMPING HAS TO STOP RIGHT NOW!"

Is the vein about to pop right out of his neck? I've never seen this shade of red on a human before, it looks like face paint!

"So, you booked a convention of blind bowlers below our high school prom? Sir, Mr. Stan, I'm so sorry, but I don't understand what you want me to do about it?"

Vein throbbing, Mr. Event Manager glares at me. "You get right up on that stage and tell everyone that I will only plug the sound system back in for the band if everyone absolutely stops jumping up and down."

"But, that's how we dance. That's dancing and this is our prom...a dance..."

"No music until everyone promises! I'm going to plug this in and I want you to take this microphone and go up there. Now."

Stan the blind bowler stands uncomfortably by his side. Really? This is REALLY happening? I've got to walk up onto that stage and tell all these people that they can't jump up and down anymore? AT PROM? Oh boy. I love a stage and I love a microphone, but I do not love this. At all.

It seems like hours have passed since the manager unplugged the band. I look out at the crowd, and it is ugly. It is a hot, sweaty sea of angry people. Where was the rest of the Prom Committee? Did anyone else come forward to stand by my side? A quick look around told me nope, just me, Karen, Junior Class President, planner of this prom.

Here I go. I see the steps leading to the stage. Move your feet Karen, you can do this. Up one, two, three steps. Turn and face the crowd. Oh boy. Take a deep breath. Why can't I feel my arms? Are my lips working right? Why are they so tingly?

"Um, hi. My name is Karen, Junior Class Officer, and we've got a situation here."

Did I really just say that? A situation? Junior Class Officer? Geez.

"So, there's a convention downstairs, right below us."

Wow, the lights were hot. I'm sweating. Oh my God, I'm sweating! Will sweat stain satin? The seniors look so, very, mad and start chanting for the music again. This isn't going well. No, not well at all.

"The convention, well they are blind bowlers. Our jumping is scaring them, so we have to stop."

"Mu-sic, mu-sic, mu-sic!"

The chanting is so loud. I search for a friendly face and find Jenny right where I left her. She gives me a thumbs up with a total look of panic on her face. Deep breath, louder voice.

"Listen, they won't let us have our music back until we promise to stop jumping."

Every single kid on the dance floor starts jumping as they continue their chant. Oh no. This is not going well. Everything's ruined. Wait, what is Mr. Senior President doing? Holy crap. He's looking right at me so of course I look behind me. Oh, hey band. Wow, the band looks angry. Breathe Karen, breathe.

He is still looking at me and he's putting his hand on the stage. Wait, is he lifting himself up onto the stage? I haven't blinked in a while. Blink Karen. He's walking towards me, and he is smiling at me. What is happening? Is anyone else seeing this? Oh wait, everyone else is seeing this. We are on the stage at prom and the band can't play and the people won't stop jumping and screaming.

Mr. Senior Class President nods at my hand. Does he see that my nail polish perfectly matches my dress which perfectly matches my shoes? Does he want to hold my hand? Here on the stage? I'm going to pass out. Then he reaches for my hand…and grabs the microphone.

"Hey! HEY! Everyone listen to me right now! We have terrified a group of innocent bowlers. Listen to Karen and STOP JUMPING."

Oh, he's powerful. Everyone listens to him, they stop jumping! He turns and smiles at me, at ME, before jumping back into the crowd.

I sidestep my way back to the stairs as the manager leads Stan the bowler back out the ballroom doors. I look up before I go down the steps and see my date in the back of the room with a fat, brown, lit cigar in his hand.

"There's my date! I'm coming for you Karen!"

So I do what any self-respecting high school junior in student government leadership would do. I drop to the floor and crawl under the nearest table. And thank you Jesus for the floor-length tablecloths my committee chose. I am totally concealed from everyone. Time to take in a deep breath and figure out what to do next. My hands are shaking, my heart is racing. Wow, it's dark in here. I've got to scoot over onto my butt and stretch out my legs in front of me. These pantyhose are so hot and wow, there's no air in here. I'm a little dizzy. Time to take these hose off. I'll just reach up and shimmy them down.

The tablecloth lifts up and Jenny dives under, knocking right into me. We burst into laughter.

"Karen! Our dates saw you, they're close! Good call hiding under here. It took me a few tables before I found you."

As her eyes adjust to the darkened, tablecloth cloaked space, she's horrified.

"What are you DOING?"

"Oh, I was so hot. That stage is hot! I'm just taking my hose off. I hate them!"

"That's not okay, pull them back up!"

"No way."

I pop off my shoes, finish the removal of the horrible hose, and sit cross-legged with my shoes next to me. Jenny is absolutely shocked that I've done such a thing. I don't even care. I've worked for months, months to plan the perfect prom. It's the only reason I ran for office. Now the whole night is blown. My weirdo date, who by the way is Jenny's date's best friend—again, is trying to find me and he's so gross. Why is he even looking for me?

"Jenny, why are the guys looking for us? I hardly even know my date. Every date I've ever had to any dance has completely blown me off."

"I mean, you looked super cute up on that stage! Your hair is perfect, and that dress is to die for. Satin and lace. The perfect combo. Your sequin bow was so sparkly up there!"

"Jenny, prom is ruined! No one will ever forget this. My God, who puts a convention of blind bowlers under a prom? What kind of event manager does that? I'm going to make some phone calls next week for sure. This is insane."

"Lighten up and put your pantyhose back on. We've got to get out of…"

The tablecloth is lifted again, and I hold my breath and shove the hose under the fluff of my dress, expecting to see my date. It's a friend from Drill Team who peers under.

"Girls, your dates are across the room again. The coast is clear!"

We crawl out from under the table, hesitatingly look around, and then stand up tall, ready to see where the night will take us.

I longingly look out at the dance floor, but feel it is too risky to go that route as my weirdo date might spot me again. And then it happens. A brown-haired cutie named John Hughes (yes, for that love of all things 80's his actual name is John Hughes) makes eye contact from the dance floor. He nods at me as he walks toward me. Then he asks me to dance with him. This is the first time a guy has wanted to dance with me. With me.

As we near the dance floor, the band changes it up. Wait, what? A slow song? A SLOW song? What do I do, what do I do, what do I do? John Hughes turns to me, I'm sure he's going to wish me well and walk away, and instead he shrugs and smiles. AGAIN! He smiles again. I don't know how it's happening, but my feet are continuing to move me forward and now I'm standing in front of him. His hands go to my waist. He is touching me and everyone around me literally disappears. It's just John Hughes, his hands on my waist, and me. I have hands too. Where are my hands supposed to go? On his shoulders. His shoulders. Got it.

What song is playing? I've got to note this song. This is epic and historic, and I have to remember it to write in my journal later tonight. Lady in Red. If only my dress was red. Then it would be perfect!

"How crazy is it that they put blind bowlers under us?"

Speak Karen.

"Oh my gosh, so crazy."

Our eyes are looking at each other. His two eyes are looking at my two eyes and I stop breathing. Inhale Karen.

"You did a really good job planning the prom."

"Thanks. I don't think the blind bowlers think so."

John Hughes is laughing. Because I said something funny. Whoa. The song is ending and he's stepping back.

"Okay, well good job!"

And just like that, John Hughes is swallowed back up into the crowd and his cool group of friends. I dive back under another table to avoid my date. And that pretty much sums up my night.

The Pact

The summer before senior year is full of shenanigans with my friends. Living just outside of Chicago, we will often pile into someone's parent's minivan and drive into the city just to drive around. If someone has money, we'll head to the iconic 1950's themed McDonald's.

There are nights when a friend asks how my mom is doing and I don't know how to answer. I am embarrassed that I don't know what to say. I usually just start to cry but once I start, I can't seem to stop. I'm sure I'm a load of fun to be with. I'm just so glad that my friends keep picking me up and inviting me to be with them. Being alone is hard and I avoid it at all costs.

Mom's health continues to remain a mystery to me. We never once sit down as a family and talk about what is happening or treatment plans. I stop asking questions that aren't given answers and I continue to live my life and keep myself very busy.

A few of us pals spend more and more time together and one night we all end up at Ted Maston's house. His parents are out of town and the night gets later and later, dwindling down to my few friends and an equal number of guys. Did I mention Ted and his friends had just graduated from high school? We are indeed in the big leagues here.

As we load the VCR with Friday the 13th I find myself next to James Davidson on the couch. There is nothing better than watching a scary movie shoulder to shoulder with a hot, older guy. I'm getting just a little bit sweaty but don't dare move away. Suddenly, his arm is around me, pulling me close—just in case I am scared. It is electric and I am thrilled. I also just enjoy the relaxing feeling of being held by someone. It doesn't hurt that he is hotter than Jake Ryan from *Sixteen Candles*!

The movie ends and it is time to head home. James stands up and I noticed we weren't the only "couple" snuggled up. We head for the door.

"Ted, that was fun. Thanks so much for the movie."

"Yeah, you're welcome. We're here all week."

Ted winks at Jenny. I look shyly at James and smile. He kind of nods and smiles back. Whoa. I think that means he likes me. I mean, he put his arm around me and that was…I mean it was… dreamy. That is the only and best word that comes to mind. We walk out the front door and huddle together as we walk to my car.

"Oh my gosh you guys, that was amazing!"

I can't keep my giggles to myself. Melanie hugs us all together.

"Thank you guys for going over there. I really like Jerry and I think he likes me back. Did you see us kiss during that one part of the movie?"

"No! What? Oh my God Melanie, that's amazing! I think he definitely likes you."

"I am so happy! Karen, James looked so into you."

"You think? Oh, I wish! Isn't he dating someone though?"

"No, I am pretty sure they broke up. Don't even think about that. No way would he put his arm around you if he was still dating her. No way."

We pile into my car and drive to my house. The girls are sleeping over. My house is the go-to because with everything going on with my mom, no one notices what I do. I don't have a curfew but that makes sense because I don't really do anything bad anyway.

We tiptoe through my house and up to my room where we all pile into my cozy nook. Jenny has an idea.

"Okay you guys, Ted said his parents are gone all week and he has the house to himself. I say we go for it with these guys. I'm into Ted, Melanie, you and Jerry are a total couple, and Karen, it looks promising for you with James. Let's make a plan. What do you think?"

Melanie practically screams, "Yes!" and I have to shush her to remind her that I do have parents asleep downstairs. I think for a minute, then answer.

"This is what I think. I think these guys are going to college in a few weeks. They are nice, and funny, and so good looking. I say we show up again tomorrow night and see what happens. Let's do this!"

I am actually kind of nervous about it all. My kissing has kind of stalled out since the big weekend of my first, and second, kisses. But what the heck? We are young, we are amazing, and these guys seem interested! Melanie has an idea.

"Let's make a pact that we will just go for it this whole week. Let's promise that we will go over to Ted's every single night and see what happens. I love you guys and this is so much fun."

Jenny is all in. I take a deep breath and push my fears aside.

"Okay, let's do it. And let's name it. We are, now and for at least the rest of this week, called The Pact."

We seal things with a formal handshake and fall asleep, needing our rest for the days to come.

And it's a good thing we got that rest because we go back to Ted's every single night of the week. Their friend group is there every night before us, drinking and doing whatever. Ted told Jenny we should wait until 10:00 or so to come over. After the older crew leaves, we run up the stairs and the guys are there waiting. It is so romantic and fun!

The guys pick a new horror movie to watch, and we all snuggle up, clinging to each other in fear. Then we all make out until late in the night and the girls sleep over at my house more than once that week.

There are so many great things about The Pact but here are the things I love the most:

1. Jenny, Melanie, and I are now so solid as friends.
2. We are having the best time!
3. James Davidson is probably the best kisser in the entire world and now my kissing skills are really epic.
4. For one whole week, I am totally distracted from Mom being sick.

The guys from The Pact go off to college and it is time to get ready for senior year of high school to begin. James gives me his address at school, and I really do plan to write him letters. Some other girls have said that he is still dating his girlfriend, but I just don't think it's true. I am going to believe he is single and that week was nothing but goodness.

I have come a long way since freshman year. I pride myself on being friends with kids in practically every group. At the end of junior year, I secured my spots on the Varsity Drill Team, Student Council, Orchesis Dance Team, and A Capella Choir. I never got an actual acting part, but I am now part of the dance crew in our school musicals. (You don't know what you're missing until you dance for a high school production of Camelot!) I happily chat with the burnouts who spend their lunch period smoking on the mall of our school campus. I like meeting all kinds of people and I especially like keeping myself very busy. If I'm ever still or quiet for too long, I get sad about my mom so I go out and find a new friend to talk to.

I decide to get active in Luther League again, and I work to renew some friendships that had faded. We have taken incredible trips and retreats in the past few years, growing in faith and friendship. I know that God is there, but we aren't really talking these days. My mom is a good person. She does a lot for everyone. She is a good mom. So why does she have cancer? I'm kind of mad at God right now. I'll keep showing up, but I am definitely mad. I don't really talk about my mom in this group, because she still doesn't want everyone to know she is sick. This is hard for me, but I am trying to be a good daughter.

Last year, I got hired at an awesome video store. My good friend Jess either quit, or got fired, I'm still not sure. But I got to replace her, and it's been a great job. Our boss, Mitch, is the uncle of my neighbor from around the corner. We are a small shop and rent VHS movies to people. Sometimes someone will come in and ask if we have Beta movies and we just try not to laugh!

A typical day on the job is I show up and the boss is there. If it's going to be a busy rental day, then either of my two other coworkers (and friends) might be there too. We tidy up the store and always have a newly released movie fired up in the VCR on the TV that hangs above the counter. It's got to be PG or G though in case kids come in. One of the best perks of this job is that we watch movies all the time. Another perk is dinner. Mitch will give one of us a $20 bill and the keys to his convertible. As a team, we decide where dinner will come from and then we get to leave work, take the awesome convertible, and drive to pick up dinner for everyone! I feel so cool driving around with the top down.

The last, and one of the best parts of the day at work, is the end of the night close out. When someone comes in to rent a movie, we fill out a slip that has the date, their name, a phone number, and the name of the movie. Before we close, I always clamor to be the one to alphabetize the slips, by last name. The movies are always due back in three days, or else they will get a late fee. When someone returns a movie, we pull out the sheets, find their name (expertly alphabetized by yours truly), and put an X through the sheet. It's a simple system that works like a charm.

We close every single night at 9:00. This is great during school because I can still go home and make phone calls. (I usually get my homework done sitting at the counter of the shop.) On weekends, it's the best because my friends will usually pick me up at 9:00 and we will go find something fun to do (hello Pact!).

Senior year...I am ready for it. I have a lot to do and a lot to look forward to.

189

Karen Cares

Service and leadership are traits both of my parents have in abundance. Growing up, I witnessed my mom and my dad serving on the boards of various organizations within our community. I loved helping my dad on stage at the big Community Chest auction. My mom's crowning glory was as chairwoman of a local fundraiser that transformed a mansion from our community and sold tickets to raise money for the benefit of children.

I watched my mom specifically and learned that she valued helping others as well as being in charge.

Throughout elementary school, if there was a project to plan, or a job to be done, I was the girl for the job. In the neighborhood, I was the second youngest kid on our half of the block but you can bet I was ringing all of the doorbells and gathering the troops every night in the summer for games of Kick the Can or Ghost in the Graveyard. I loved being in charge and encouraging my friends and neighbors to have fun and do well.

I want my mom to be proud of the leader I am becoming. It is time to focus my planning on my ultimate prize in leadership— Senior Class President. I put together an amazing slate of some of my best friends who show leadership across sports and clubs. Dan, my locker neighbor, and total secret crush, is a baseball player, good student, and also in A Capella Choir, and will make the best VP to my President. Heather and Amanda are dependable, kind, smart, and good friends who round out our ticket as Treasurer and Secretary. They are all willing to serve with me and agree to go for it.

My slogan is Karen Cares, because let me tell you, in my mind, no one cares more about the well-being of our class than I do. My main, and secret, reason for running is to plan our ten-year class reunion in 1998. I know I am the woman for the job and last year's prom had been a slam dunk (well, except for the blind bowler debacle). I am excited but also nervous.

I have two opponents. Rod is a star athlete and is well-liked and well-known in our very large senior class. Paul is a bit of a class clown and has chosen to run as a joke. He even brags about how he is running as a spoiler and doesn't care. Paul and I have the same larger friend group and I try to convince him to withdraw his nomination, so we won't split the vote. He laughs and says he doesn't care. But I care. Karen Cares is my slogan after all.

My campaign team makes countless posters and cuts out Karen Cares buttons to be worn on the chests of as many classmates as possible. I am told by a guy friend that Rod decided to spread some ugly rumors about me in the gym locker room. Any guy who knows me knows that they can't possibly be true because I can't even get a willing date to a dance for goodness sake. But I feel the alleged rumors are doing some damage.

The election comes and goes and Rod wins. But the kicker here is that he won, along with the rest of my slate. I am crushed in so many ways. Rod allegedly lied about me and still won.

I really wanted that win to show my parents that I can be a top leader. Because my mom's cancer is now spreading to other parts of her body, I'm not even sure they realize I ran, and lost, a big election. As her cancer spreads, her treatments continue, and my mom shuts down even more. She doesn't talk about what is happening and still doesn't want people to know.

I was convinced a win, and the title of Senior Class President, would have boosted her morale and she might see me and be proud.

Senior Year Homecoming

Jenny is absolutely my best friend, and I am spending most of my waking hours at her house. Her parents are so kind, and I feel like I am always welcome there. Jenny is so pretty, always seems to have a boyfriend, and those tend to be the guys we hang out with on the weekends. I'm not going to lie, every single time I get ready to go out, I have high hopes for some kind of love connection and a boyfriend of my own. Unfortunately for Homecoming this year, none of Jenny's boyfriends' friends are possibilities for me as a date.

I tap into what I know and find anyone to help set me up with a guy from another school. Once again, I will pay for the ticket to the dance, I will pay for the limo, I will pay for dinner…just please, for the love of all things, someone go with me to my senior Homecoming.

Success! I'm set up with a guy from Hinsdale Central and we chat on the phone a few times before the dance. He is a year younger, and I'm told he's very good looking. As an "older woman," I feel like I just might have a chance at a boyfriend this time. I've got a lot going for me and I hope he sees it.

It's now Homecoming week, and as an involved senior, it is an absolute blast. Student Council has added so many activities including a whole carnival! As I sit here in the dunk tank, looking out over the fieldhouse carnival set-up, I am crazy proud of all the hard work we did to make such a fun day for the kids in the community. I love being busy and laughing as much as I can. Helping to plan this carnival seriously helped and I'm going to be sad when it's all over.

"Modder! You're toast! I'm going to dunk you!"

Jenny throws a ball at the target and misses.

"Nice try! Ha! Wait…what are you doing?"

Jenny is running full speed ahead at the target.

SPLASH

I emerge from the cold water, rub the water from my eyes, and laugh my head off.

"Nice! You goon!"

With the carnival wrapping up, I've still got the game and the dance to look forward to. Senior year is awesome!

I love that our high school has varsity football games on Saturday afternoons. Our Drill Team is gathered together before the game getting a pep talk from our captains.

"Let's rock this girls. We are the Varsity Drill Team and we are the best! Let's have fun!"

We perform the school fight song and a show-stopping kick routine for half-time. I love every second on the field with my teammates and friends. I don't love our psycho coach on the sidelines. We call her Scary Sherrie because she is so intense. Doesn't she know high school is supposed to be fun?

After the game, I race home and start to get ready for the dance. A quick shower and then I start on my hair. I blow-dry it and put my hair into the fanciest style I can—a headband French braid, with the end tucked behind my ear. Then I use the smallest wand curling iron in existence to curl the ends of the rest of my hair. Oh, and my bangs, well, they are an actual masterpiece. Tightly curled, then teased to perfection, and sprayed to a state of complete immobilization.

Make-up: start with a layer of Oil of Olay to keep my skin looking young and fresh. Mom has taught me to always moisturize, and I do. I'm lucky my skin is so clear, and I plan on keeping it that way. Maybe my date will get up close and personal, and I want my face to be soft and inviting. I sharpen my eyeliner and carefully frame my top lid and then go to the bottom. I stopped wearing it on the inside of my lower eyelid ledge a couple of years ago. This way makes my eyes so much brighter. Eye shadow, blush, lip gloss. I look good.

Time for my dress and this dress is EVERYTHING. I bought it from the Jessica McClintock store in Water Tower Place, downtown Chicago. It has long-sleeved black velvet on top, with a hot pink, drop waist taffeta, tea length skirt. On my hip is a gorgeous pink bow, as stiff as my perfect bangs. Sheer black hose and black, patent leather, pointed toe flats topped with hot pink bows that CLIP ON to my shoes. Absolute perfection.

I spritz on some Lily of the Valley perfume from Crabtree & Evelyn and make my way downstairs. Mom is so happy that I have a date and my whole family is home. Both of my parents tell me I look pretty and then we head to the front room to wait for my date. Dad is the first to spot him as he turns onto our street.

"Oh boy, I think that's him! Look at that car. Is that? Is that a Jaguar?"

He pulls into the driveway.

"Holy smokes, he's driving a Jaguar! That's the big time. Rich Hinsdale kid! Way to go, Karen!"

"Dad, geez! Who cares what car he drives?"

"But a Jaguar! Okay, be cool, he's getting out of his car."

"Oh, he's handsome."

"Mom, don't be a weirdo."

"But he is!"

She giggles as my date walks towards the front door.

"Everyone, be cool!"

The doorbell rings. I descend the stairs to open it and get a quick glance in the hallway mirror as I go. I look good. It's going to be a good night. I open the door. He is handsome. I let him in and we take a few pictures. He's kind of quiet but he's nice to look at so I don't mind that very much. As the limo pulls up to pick us up and take us to our next stop, my dad jumps in.

"Oh, now you'd better leave your car keys with us. We might need to move the car around and such."

"Sure, here you go Mr. Modder. We'll see you all later."

I have high hopes for a possible boyfriend in this guy and leave for the dance full of good thoughts and dreams of kissing his cute face.

Unfortunately, even though he is from another school, several towns away, he knows a lot of kids from my school. Once we walk in the doors to the high school, he bolts, and I only see him again at the end of the night when my dad picks us up and brings us back to our house so he can drive himself home.

After he leaves, Dad asks how the night was.

"I don't really want to talk about it. He basically ditched me and hung out with friends he has that I didn't know about. I think he kind of used me to go to the dance."

"That's too bad. If it makes you feel any better, after you left, your sister and I took his car for a joyride around the neighborhood. It didn't run that great."

"Dad!!"

I can't help but laugh. Another night of hopes and dreams for a good night kiss dashed by yet another setup. I've got two dances left in high school. Maybe, just maybe, I'll get a willing date for one of them.

Something is Going to Break

Jenny and I have both decided to go to Bradley University for college! Bradley's just a couple of hours away from Chicago in central Illinois. We visited three colleges together and didn't really talk about it with each other. The other day I asked her what she was thinking, and she said Bradley! I told her I picked Bradley too and then we both decided not to be roommates. This way, we could meet new people and have a chance at really building new friendships. Dad went to Bradley too and he is so proud and excited for me. Mom and Dad both think it's a good idea that Jenny and I have other roommates. I hope we get good ones!

With college plans secure, I spend my time at Drill Team or Orchesis practice, work, or my friend's houses. Life at home is heavy. Mom seems to always be in bed or upset. No one really asks about what I am doing. I am just trusted to be making wise decisions. Honestly, I am doing a good job. I am not a big drinker, instead I choose to drive a lot so my friends can drink whatever they secure from their parent's collections, or local liquor stores who easily sell to teenagers. I also notice that when I drink, I tend to get sad and cry. That doesn't feel good, and I want to avoid that as much as possible.

I keep busy, I try to laugh a lot, and I try not to cry. When I start to cry, I have a really hard time turning it off again. So it's best if I hold it in and fight against it. Holding it in makes me tired though. I'm starting to feel a lot of pressure. I'm afraid something's going to go sideways in my life so I work hard to keep control over everything I can.

Our Drill Team is a well-known, award-winning team. Our coach, Scary Sherrie, is definitely intense. We practice daily and part of our warm up is to be in our kick line and do 500 straight kicks in a row and if anyone, I mean anyone, stops smiling, she stops us and we have to start again. She says we should put Vaseline on our teeth to keep the smile cemented. Some girls do not want to do that. I love to kick, and actually usually enjoy this part of practice. Smiling here is easy for me.

I am starting to notice that some girls (our team is quite large) break and run to vomit in the nearby bathroom during kick practice. And sometimes, they don't always make it to the bathroom. There is no mercy from our coach and the team of captains are dedicated and hell bent on a state title.

I find my days drifting through classes at school, going straight to practice, which is now becoming far from fun, going straight to work at the video store, and then home to a depressing house. It is really starting to wear on me.

One day I have had enough. I decide to quit the Drill Team. At my high school, this is unheard of. Being on Varsity Drill Team is a major accomplishment, a coveted position. Girls on the Freshman and JV teams work hard with the hopes of making Varsity as a junior. I worked hard to make JV last year and was so glad to make

Varsity this year. But it is just too much. Practices are full of tears and I only have room for keeping busy and laughing. Not what this has become.

I walk off and it feels like a great relief. Within the week, twelve more girls leave the team. I become a bit of a hero and the other girls who quit thank me for paving the way. That feels weird. Some of my really good friends are leaders of the team and I never thought so many other girls would quit. Now we have no chance at a state title. I feel badly for letting down my friends down. I also know that if I didn't quit something, I wouldl soon break from the pressure building in my life.

In the weeks after quitting, lots of kids are high-fiving me in the hallway. They think I'm some sort of champion for leaving such a popular team. A lot of recreational softball teams are forming and I end up on a team with all of the other girls who quit. They pick the name Mod Squad and I'm this weird hero I never wanted to be.

I feel like I've let people down. I will miss performing and basketball games are so fun because the crowd is so close. I won't miss Scary Sherrie, and I won't miss my friends throwing up all over the place. It just doesn't feel good to not finish what I started.

Comfort

"Karen!"

I am up in my room, rearranging the pillows in the cozy nook I created for myself. Over in the smaller section of my L-shaped room, there are built-in bookshelves. Next to that I have my white, plastic, stackable shelves. I broke the shelves up so there would be two on either side of the built-ins. My TV is on the top over on the right side. Across from all the shelving, and pushed up against the wall, under the windows, is the inflatable double mattress that I bought with my own money. I wrapped it in the bright yellow blanket from my bed. The blanket is soft with a silky section at the top, by my face. But here, the silky part is tucked back, up against the wall. Then, carefully placed all around the back and side are my prized possession—my pillows.

These pillows aren't just any pillows. I bought each one with money earned from babysitting, and then my job at the video store. I only bought the primary-colored ones and put them in the order of the rainbow. I bought enough to fill the whole cozy nook. Maybe my favorite thing about the pillows is that I bought them all at our family's favorite store, Marshall Field's.

Marshall Field's has a store in Oak Park! It is my mom's favorite place to shop. We park over on the side in a parking lot and enter the store through their BAKERY! My mom buys me a chocolate long john every time we go through. It smells like chocolate, vanilla, sugar, and goodness. Then through the bakery, downstairs, is the housewares department and all of the glorious pillows that I love so much. Mom hasn't taken me to Marshall Field's in a while.

I am busy straightening and fluffing when Mom calls out, kind of quietly.

"Yeah Mom?"

I go downstairs and find her sitting at the kitchen table, her usual spot by the phone. There are dark circles under her eyes. I can feel how tired she is. I wonder what made her so tired. No one really tells me much of anything regarding her treatments. Should I ask? No, it will probably be too hard for her to talk about it.

"Karen, I need you to look at the list."

The list is all my mom's jewelry, divided up between my sister, brother, and me. She has been asking us to look at the list, on our own, and let her know we are good with her choices. It lives on her little desk area in our kitchen. I see it there, every day. It is folded up and small, but in my eyes, it is a gigantic, brightly lit, smoldering paper of badness.

"Mom. I don't need to look at it."

I can't look at her. I do not want to ever look at that list. Looking at the list is admitting that my mom is going to die.

"Karen."

"Mom."

"It's important."

My sister looked and she was fine with it. My brother looked— no issues. Up until now, I refused to look at the list. I dug in my heels and absolutely refused. Which, sadly, made everyone angry. No one figured out that maybe, just maybe, a teenager wasn't prepared to agree to the list because then it just might give her mom permission to die.

I was not going to look at that list. Mom hands it to me, and I begrudgingly take it up to my room. I set it down on my dresser, as far away from my cozy nook as it can go.

I hate this list. My sister is outright angry with me for my refusal to read it. My brother is frustrated because I'm not being cooperative. They think our mom isn't asking for much, so why can't I look and give my agreement?

Why can't anyone understand why I don't want to look?

I have said over and over that I am sure everything is fine, there is no need for any of us to even look. Whatever she decides would be fine. Fine, just fine.

I am quite certain everyone thinks I am being a difficult teenager. I guess I am. I'm also quite certain that no one thinks it is a big deal. I still don't understand how no one seems to see my perspective. I want to be left alone. I don't want to read the list. I don't want to agree to inheriting jewelry. I don't want my mom to die.

I don't say that out loud. No one asked. I feel like there is just anger and so, I walk over to my dresser, and read the list.

My eyes are blurring from tears as I unfold the list and scan it. Against everything screaming within me, I read it. Then I fold it back up as I wipe the stupid tears off my face. I look around my room full of rainbows and colors and light. I want to stay up here with all of my things and never leave.

I bring the list back down to my mom and set it next to her on the table.

"Are you good with it?

A voice is screaming within my head. No! I am not good with any of it.

"Susan is the oldest and that's why she gets my diamond set. David will get my engagement ring and wedding band so he can give it to his bride someday."

I want to scream, "I KNOW! I JUST READ THE DAMN LIST!" Instead, I look at the floor.

"And he gets all of my gold jewelry because those will be good gifts for her too. I want you to have all of my birthstone jewelry and that includes a ring Dad gave me when we were dating…"

I want to run out the door and down the block and I want to keep running. Instead, I inhale and keep looking at the floor.

"And I want you to have my pearl necklace. Susan got one from Peter as a wedding gift so she won't need it, but she will get the bracelet and then you can have the earrings."

Her voice is pretty quiet at this point. My rage is simmering to just plain fear. I look up and nod.

"Fine."

I turn and go back up to my room and lay face down on my bed. I stretch out my arms to hold onto the cloud bedspread that Mom made for me to match my rainbow room. I curl my afghan close. I breathe it in, hugging the love she poured into it when she made it for me.

I cry by myself. I feel that I can't share my sadness or feelings anywhere at home because I will make my mom feel worse when she is already so sick. I am so lonely.

I turn over onto my back and stare up at my ceiling. I cover myself up with the afghan and remember when I was a little girl and Mom called me to her room.

"Karen, it's time for me to make your afghan. What colors would you like me to use?"

"Oooo, it's my turn? How about blue and yellow and white to match my room?"

At the time, my room was downstairs and had light blue wallpaper with mushrooms and flowers. Sue's room was upstairs, and her walls were green, so her afghan was yellow and green and pink. David had the God-bless-America-room so his was red and white and blue. They are all the perfect size to cover up a kid and it is finally my turn!

I calm down. I realize that even though no details are really shared about the extent of her illness, it must be pretty bad if she's making lists.

A piece of my spirit breaks as I curl up and quietly sob into my afghan.

Friendships and Celebrations

I can honestly say that I am surviving my senior year because I have the best friends in the whole world.

When things at home are a struggle, I am welcomed into the homes of my friends and their families. I spend hours and hours on the phone, with that cord stretched taut from the hallway to my bedroom. If I can't use the phone, I'll pour out my heart on a piece of notebook paper and fold it up to be hand delivered to a friend at school the next morning. We stuff notes through locker vents, hand off in the hallway, and even pass them during our classes. Bottom line—communication with my friends is my lifeline.

My 18th birthday is here. I always have a friend party and a family party with menus of my choosing. I worry that this year won't happen but, in the end, my senior year is no exception. It is a time I will always cherish. The friends I invite are all thoughtful, caring, and so much fun. They aren't all necessarily close friends with each other, but they each mean something to me, and I really love each friend that comes for my party. I am so lucky!

It's a Saturday, just after my birthday. I'm heading over to Melanie's house, another house that I really like to spend time at. Her big family lives in a gorgeous home with a big wrap-around porch. We usually get snacks and hunker down in the TV room watching movies, gossiping, and laughing our heads off. I'm getting ready up in my room and all of a sudden, my door bursts open.

"What on earth?!"

Two of my friends bound into my room.

"We are here to kidnap you!"

What is going on???

"Are you serious?"

"Yes! Let's go!"

They grab my arm and pull me down the stairs. Mom is standing in the hallway with a big smile. She knew they were coming!

"Thanks, Mrs. Modder! We will have her back home late tonight! Don't wait up!"

We're through the house, out the door, and Jenny pulls out a bandana and blindfolds me. I am excited and nervous, joyful and terrified. What are these friends of mine up to? We drive for a while and get out of the car. Someone holds my hand as I am led up a sidewalk.

"You guys! What is going on?!"

Lots of giggling and I can hear hushed voices as I hold my breath, wondering what on earth is happening. We stop walking. The blindfold is ripped away and a collective, "Surprise!" rings out. I can't breathe. I can't speak. My breath is literally taken away from me.

My eyes adjust and I look up at Melanie's front porch. It is full of a huge variety of friends and they are cheering, whistling, and clapping—to celebrate me. I feel the love and support of friends.

"Get up here, Karen!"

I walk up the steps and hug everyone I can touch. Melanie and I are such good friends and she nailed it by inviting all kinds of people to this party. This party for me!! I can't even believe it.

"You are all here for me? For my birthday? Thank you!"

More kids are inside and I am pretty sure there are several here for a good party and have no idea it is for my birthday! As Melanie, Jenny, and I walk into the house, everyone follows and they start to tell me to open my gifts.

"Gifts? Are you kidding me? You got me gifts?"

And oh, there are gifts. Gag gifts, and they are maybe the best part of the night. Jenny and Carrie (my kidnappers) got me a six foot tall, giant, inflatable Gumby! Chrissy hands me a gift and I open it next. I tear off the comic book paper and open the box—it's one of the horrible bathing suits from school!

"Chrissy! How did you get this???"

"I took one!"

"No way! You stole a school bathing suit for me? You are amazing!"

206

Then my good guy friends hand me a grocery bag.

"We picked this out special just for you."

I look in the bag and cannot even believe how ugly my gift is.

"What the hell is this???"

"It's a beautiful dress from Goodwill. Just for you!"

I pull it out of the bag and everyone in the house bursts into laughter. It is a long, polyester dress, from probably the 1960's, with large, bright flowers all over it.

"I love it!"

Someone grabs it from me and starts to dress Gumby in it.

"It's perfect!"

I cannot believe this is my life and these are my friends. If the purpose of this party is to make me laugh and feel loved by my friends, well, it worked.

Turning 18 is momentous.

Spring Showcase

Since quitting Drill Team, life definitely seems a little smoother. I still get to perform with Orchesis and our Spring Showcase is coming up. I still can't believe I made Orchesis junior year, and I pinch myself almost every day at rehearsals. There is something so special about the dance studio at school. Ms. Marcham is the absolute greatest. She is so happy and upbeat. She plays the best music, and she really encourages every single one of us. Of course, the best dancers are front and center—they should be. I'm just so happy to be on the stage with them.

The theme of this year's show is: Chicago. Ms. Marcham assigns us to the dances, chooses the music, and then we choreograph. I'm in more this year than last and it feels so good. I have 9th period off, because I'm finally a senior and Orchesis counts as a team. After 8th period, every single day, I go to the dance locker room and change into dance clothes.

My favorite dance outfits right now come from the Leo's factory outlet in Chicago. It's right by my house! I could spend all of my money there. I've got a deep purple, ribbed, tank unitard with stirrups (duh), a fabulous two-piece lavender and light green vertical striped ensemble, and I love my black dance pants that are kind of like parachute pants but for dancers. Once I'm in my dance clothes, I seriously feel like the hottest shit to come out of the locker room. I grab my backpack and head to the fieldhouse where all of the other senior athletes are congregating, doing homework, and goofing around. I like to sit right on the center of the basketball court and stretch with my friends while we do homework and talk. I am so flexible and stretching is my favorite thing right now. I can sit in any of the splits and that helps my leaps and kicks to be some of the best in the group.

Bottom line, I feel like I belong with this crew and I am so glad to be here.

Now here we are, opening night of Chicago: Orchesis Showcase 1987-88. For the first time in a long time, my mom is planning to come and see me perform. I bought tickets for my parents and know this is a difficult outing for her to navigate. Her weakness and the extent of her illness is way more evident when she goes out of the house.

I am in the opening number. Ms. Marcham comes to the green room and tells us all to take our places in the wings for the first number. It's showtime! I'm nervous and excited. I didn't tell my parents what my character is in this first number about the streets of Chicago. I'm a prostitute! I'm wearing a leopard print leotard, black fishnet tights, and black character shoes. My hair is teased super high and my make-up screams 'hooker-on-the-streets.' I giggle as I walk to the stage. I take a minute to lean against the wall and stretch each leg up over my head before taking my spot right at the curtain.

I peek out to see my folks and notice their seats are empty. My heart sinks and then suddenly, I see another couple come in and sit in my parent's seats. They were the last to sit and the house lights start to dim. Those are my parents' seats and I don't know what to do. Why aren't they here? Who are those people?

I start to panic as I now watch my parents enter the darkened theater. My dad starts helping my mom navigate the steep stairs as they descend to their row, right in the center of the theater, best seats in the actual house. When they get to the row, my mom is obviously winded and leaning into my dad. Someone else is in their seats!

I start to leave the wings and my friends hold me back and point out that our director is heading to the situation and will smooth things over. The house lights come on. I hold my breath.

My heart is pounding, and tears are threatening my stage make-up. It is a good thing Ms. Marcham sorts it out and gets my parents into their seats because I can only imagine the actual shock to the entire audience if I popped out of the wings in my fishnets and cut over the hip leopard leotard! The house lights go down, and the music starts. I pat my swelling tears back and take the stage. I dance for my mom, and it feels incredible to know she is there. I want her to see me and to be proud.

Senior Prom

My friends and I begin hanging around with a group of guys from St. Pat's, a Catholic high school in Chicago. It is just far enough from home to make it all very exotic and exciting.

A brown haired, brown eyed stud named Marco catches my eye, and along with others in the group, we couple off. For weeks now, I am making out with Marco on the regular and Senior Prom is on the horizon.

Could it actually be that I might be dating a hot guy from Chicago and might have a willing date to a dance—to my senior prom?

Time passes and our weekends are so much fun, hanging out and making out with the Chicago crowd. As talks of prom draw closer, my hopes are high and I am having fun with this new group of friends.

One day, it all crashes around me. I find out that Marco asked another girl—from my school—to his prom. What on earth? I thought everything was going so well. Apparently not. Suddenly Marco isn't able to talk on the phone, and the other guys aren't talking to me.

I finally get hold of Marco, via our landline, for an explanation.

"Marco, hi. How are you?"

"Um, hey Karen. Yeah, fine, I guess."

"I heard you asked Stephanie to your prom."

"Uh, yeah."

"I thought we were cool."

"Yeah, we were, I mean, we are."

"Then why Stephanie? I was thinking you and I might go to both of our proms."

"About that. Listen, I'm going to be honest with you."

"I would hope so."

"Me and the guys have a bet."

"What kind of bet?"

"Geez. Me and the guys have a bet about who can get laid on prom night."

"And…"

"And, Stephanie is kind of a sure thing."

"Are you kidding me?"

"No. Look, I'm sorry. I am. I like hanging out with you. But this is with the guys. You know, senior prom stuff."

"Oh, I know. I'm not going to lie. This sucks. I really liked you Marco."

"Yeah, you're nice and all too. Okay. Bye."

Click.

I sit on the floor of my room, looking at the phone. I can't believe this! Now what am I going to do? I thought Marco was a sure bet for a date and it would actually be fun. I call Melanie because she's 'dating' one of the other guys.

"Hi, is Melanie there?"

Melanie picks up.

"Melanie! I just talked to Marco. He said he didn't want to go with me to prom because the guys have a bet! Stephanie is a 'sure thing.' What the hell? What are you doing to do?"

She's silent for a bit.

"I'm going with Jeff to prom."

"Are you kidding me? You are?"

"Yeah, I really like Jeff. I think he's the one. And listen, don't be upset. Jeff told me Marco respects you too much and that's why he didn't ask you."

"Great. That makes me feel a whole lot better. I've got to go. Bye."

I hang up and just lay flat out on my back looking at the ceiling of my room. This is the last dance of my high school career. This was going to be different. I was going to have a willing date. And now…nothing. My life sucks!

Whatever Marco, I hope you don't catch an STD on prom night.

I need a date, and this is getting depressing. Amanda thinks she has a contender, a friend of her date. Again, the weird friend of a best friend's date. Is this to be my legacy? But desperate times, right?

His name is Matt. It seems as if he is willing. He is a year younger than me and goes to yet another local high school. I'm sure he thinks the idea of another prom will be fun. Phone numbers are exchanged and I begin my final campaign as a high school senior to secure a date to a dance.

We start talking on the phone. Matt is nice and he is funny. We have never physically met, have no idea what the other looks like, and he accepts my invite to the dance.

I have a date to senior prom.

Mom is very happy that I have a date. As I understand it, at this point her cancer has spread to her bones and maybe her eyes. The details are vague, and I am expected to contribute at home, lay low, and I feel like people want me to stay out of the way.

Matt and I continue our regular phone calls after school and sometimes at work at the video store. He is actually a really good guy. He probably looks like a troll or something and that's why he's being nice me.

The day of the dance is here. I go to Jenny's house to get ready. We do our own hair and make-up, and we are both borrowing dresses from her glamorous mom. Mine is a stunning peach silk, strapless, tea length, drop-waist number with a bow of the same fabric prominent on the waistline, large rhinestones adding extra flair on the knot of the bow. I went back to Baker's for the ever-important matching shoe and purse dye job.

Jenny and I aren't in the same group for this dance, and we are bummed. But I feel beautiful and head home where Matt will be picking me up. Mom is in the hospital right now for what I only know are cancer complications. She won't be there for the pictures or anything.

I am about to finally meet Matt in person and see if he is a troll, or as cute as he sounds on the phone.

My older sister volunteered to order and pick up the boutonniere. I told her to make sure it matches my peach dress. My dad has the camera ready and there will be extra pictures taken for Mom to see.

The doorbell rings. I hold my breath, walk carefully down the steps, and open the door. Matt is as cute as he sounded. Breathless, I invite him in and walk quickly through the house to get his boutonniere from the refrigerator. I don't want to leave him with Dad and Sue for too long. Dad has already probably secured his car keys for a spin around the block later! I am so excited for the promise of this night. I open the fridge, grab the flower box, and look inside. I gasp. Really loudly.

Inside the box is a fresh giant white carnation and tucked into the exact center is a delicate peach rosebud. The boutonniere looks exactly, I mean exactly, like a boob. In a panic, I call my sister into the kitchen and demand an explanation for this breast I am to pin on my super cute date's lapel.

"This is a boob, Sue. A BOOB! What am I supposed to do with this!"

She is trying really hard not to laugh and I am trying really hard not to cry.

"Hmmm, it does kind of look like a boob."

"Sue! It is a complete and total boob and when he sees it he is not going to want to have anything to do with me! It is my senior prom for God's sake! It's a boob!"

I look at her. She looks right back. And then I burst into fits of laughter. We calm down.

"Listen, Kar, he probably won't even notice. Now let's go pin it on him so you're not late to Amanda's house."

We walk back to the front room. Matt tries to pin a beautiful flower arrangement to my dress but his hands are shaking.

His hands are shaking! Why is he nervous? Geez, he's cute. Focus, Karen. Time to pin on his boob, I mean, boutonniere.

As I pin it on, I quietly apologize, and he just laughs and goes with it. What a relief. It appears as though my blind date is indeed nice, funny, and cute. As I float to his car, I wave at Dad and in a not quiet voice, we both hear my dad say, "Well, they're off like a prom dress." Matt grabs my hand and laughs some more. We drive to meet up with the rest of our group at Amanda's house. It's a mix of his friends and mine. Amanda's mom serves champagne. What a night this is shaping up to be!

Matt and I continue to hit it off. We pile into taxis to transport us to prom. Four of us are kind of jammed in the backseat and so I'm kind of half sitting on Matt's lap. I sneak a look at him right as he turns his gorgeous face towards mine. And then he kisses me. My stomach does a flip and I think it might be the best kiss I have ever kissed. Then he kisses me again and it's a for real, passionate kiss.

What is this madness? I am so happy and giggly and I just want to keep kissing this blind date of mine. I've gotten an actual unsolicited kiss before we even get to the dance. Every missed dance, and all the heartache from never being chosen as a date disappears. It melts away on the lips of blind-date-Matt in the back of a taxi on the way to senior prom in Chicago.

The dance is everything I dream a high school dance could be, and more. We arrive at the venue and ride an escalator down to the action. I stand in front of my handsome date and lean into him. He kisses me again on the way down. Am I dreaming? Near the bottom, we are greeted by a bunch of my friends shouting, "Karen!" It is a wonderful feeling of belonging.

Matt actually appears to be glad to be my date and spends the entire night dancing and talking to me. While I thoroughly enjoyed planning prom last year, this is a whole new level of fun. There don't seem to be any blind bowlers below us and my date, for the first time ever, is into me. I float through the night, with my date by my side, stealing kisses whenever we can.

The next day, our small group of six follows tradition and heads to the family lake house of one of the guys in our group. Four of us drive in someone's convertible, and that feels fancy! Matt and I are comfortably snuggled in the back seat and we laugh the whole ride there.

Is this really my weekend? I am in stunned disbelief.

Once we arrive at the cabin, it isn't quite warm enough to swim, but definitely warm enough to don our swimsuits and hang out in the sun for a while. I am prepared for this. All of my time spent doing high kicks and dancing prepped my bod for my epic one-piece, strapless, cut over the hip, suit.

Did I mention the entire center is cut out, baring my well-toned abs? How I love this suit. Matt seems to like it as well. We spend every moment together. We play games, we eat food, we talk, we laugh. At one point, we are even making out on the floor underneath a ping-pong table. I've come a long way in my under-a-ping-pong-table games! It is amazing!

The best part of this post-prom day trip to the lake is the sheer joy I feel, escaping from "real life" and literally laughing all day.

Graduations

Just a few weeks later, our family has two graduations to celebrate. My brother is graduating from college with plans to head to veterinary school and his graduation is first. Mom is really weak. She wants to go to the graduation and my brother works with the local branch of The American Cancer Society to secure a wheelchair. It is scary that she needs a wheelchair.

After we arrive, I vividly see how fragile she has become and for the first time, I am fearful that she might die from this cancer that has interfered so savagely with our lives. For me, his graduation day is tense and fraught with worry. I watch as my mom struggles to be comfortable, to breathe, to have the energy to be present and enjoy the occasion. She wears a favorite dress of hers—navy, past the knee, flared at the bottom, with white trim, almost a nautical theme. It is a special dress for a special day.

His graduation weekend takes a toll on her physically. Later that week, she is admitted to the hospital with my high school graduation just days away. I approach Dad with some questions. He looks tired.

"Dad, how long do you think Mom will be in the hospital?"

"I don't know."

"Do you think there's a chance she will be out and able to come to my graduation?"

"I don't know."

"I went to my dean and found out there is special wheelchair seating. It's on the track, right on the field. I got tickets there for you and Mom."

"I don't know if she will be home."

"Well just in case, you have the special seating. Your name is on a list, and you just follow signs for handicapped seating. Okay?"

"Thank you, honey."

"You're welcome. I love you Dad. I sure hope Mom can come."

"I hope so too."

"I got my dress."

"Okay, that's good."

A long-standing tradition at my public high school is for the girls to wear long white dresses, carry red roses, and for the boys wear dark suits with red ties. Finding a long white dress, that no one else bought, is the goal.

My friends and their moms shopped together, and I was devastated to be accomplishing this important task on my own. I waited too long and bought literally whatever was left. It's graduation day, and Mom is still in the hospital, unable to attend. I know she is sad to miss it. I am even more sad.

I am angry that my brother's graduation took so much of her energy that she can't come to mine. It was a long drive, a hotel, eating our meals out, going to the college, using the wheelchair, then driving home. It was too much and now she can't be at my graduation. It sucks and is so unfair.

I am angry my mom isn't here to help me get ready, to see me, to think I look beautiful in a dress we shopped for together.

I am angry that my friends all have stunning gowns that their moms helped them find. I hug everyone and tell them how much I will miss them when we all go to college.

As we process into the stadium, I scan the handicapped section of seating, just in case my family is able to surprise me and get her here. I want to see her there so desperately. Nothing else matters.

She isn't there. She is in the hospital. I think she is dying. I am sad and I am scared as I sit in my folding chair on the football field.

God, is it too much to ask that you heal my mom? She got to go to David's graduation. Mine is important too. Why does she have to be so sick? She is nice and she is funny, and she helps kids. She always goes to church, and I don't understand.

My family tries. My dad and siblings are somewhere in the stadium. When my name is called, and I walk across the stage to get my diploma, in my slightly wrinkled gown, they cheer maybe louder than any other group in the stadium and that makes me smile. They see me.

It's now the day after graduation and Matt is going to drive over because he has something for me. I see him pull up in his car. He can't stay, so I go out to meet him. He is so cute and that smile… ugh. I melt when I see that smile.

"Hey!"

He gets out of the car and walks around to lean on the passenger door. Just like Jake Ryan at the end of Sixteen Candles. Dream.

"Hey."

He puts his hand out and takes mine. Then he pulls me into him and kisses me. Holy smokes he is a good kisser. He kisses me right there on the street for everyone to see! Wow. Then he reaches into the window of his car.

"I got you something for graduation."

"You really didn't have to."

"I know. But I won't be here for your party and well, I wanted you to have this before I leave for my trip."

He hands me a small, wrapped gift, shaped exactly like a cassette tape.

"Hmmm, I wonder what this could be?"

We look at each other and both laugh. His eyes are sparkly. My stomach does a flip.

"I can't believe we are both going to be in Europe on two totally separate school trips at the same time. It would be so fun if we could be there at the same time."

I unwrap the cassette, look at it, then back up into those dreamy eyes.

"There is a song on here and every single time I hear it, I think of you."

He turns the cassette over and points.

"In Your Eyes. You have the most incredible eyes."

"Wow."

This is even better than the Jake Ryan moment!

"Thank you."

"I thought it could be our song. We can both listen to it when we are on our trips and think of each other. Then we won't feel so far away from each other."

Then he leans in and gives me another kiss and I think I have just melted right into my front lawn.

"Wow."

"I have to go. I'll see you in a couple of weeks, okay?"

"Yes, that is definitely okay. Thank you for coming over. This is the best gift ever."

Graduation Party

My mom threw big grad parties for my older siblings. My sister's party even had a live band in the garage. It was a big bash with family, friends, music, and food. My brother didn't want a band, but his party was as big, full of his baseball friends, neighbors, family, and friends.

My party is going to be smaller, and it is just assumed I will understand and be okay with it. My mom is in the hospital still so my Uncle Ron will videotape the entire party for her to watch when she comes home.

The party is underway. Uncle Ron loves his video camera that rests on his shoulder and I can tell he enjoys walking around the party, filming for Mom to see. It's just family, no friends. We all have to be upbeat and show how much fun we are having so she can see it.

I resent that the party isn't for me at all. I love my mom, and I am devastated that she couldn't plan my party, shop for it, cook, and be here. It is absolutely not the same without my mom, the life of the party, here to share it with me.

Mid-June 1988

Mom is still in the hospital since just after Dave's graduation. I go to visit her pretty much every day.

"How's the packing going Karen?"

"Mom, it's going well. I am bringing almost all Multiples. I got them at Marshall Field's and they are so awesome. They say I can roll them up and they won't get wrinkled at all. Isn't that perfect? I've got skirts, pants, tops, jumpsuits, and the coolest thing is the belts! They can scrunch up and be a belt, or you can have them be a tube top, or the best part—they can be pulled tight and act as a mini skirt! I love them! I got them in lots of fun colors but also white and black to go with all the colors. I wish you could have gone shopping with me for them. You'll love them. They are comfy too!"

I look over at Mom and she's sound asleep.

"Aw Mom, I wish you could have gone shopping with me. I miss shopping with you so much. I wish you could come home, and I wish you'd get better."

My voice drops to a whisper as I hold her hand.

"Mom, I wish you never got cancer. I am going to pray for you every day when I am gone. I don't even want to go but Dad said I must. He said I can't call home either. Mom, that's going to be hard. I love you Mom and I'm going to miss you so much."

I kiss her on the forehead and head for the door.

"Have fun, Karen. Have fun for me."

"I will Mom. I love you!"

"I love you too."

I gulp air into my lungs as I leave her hospital room.

I have been excited for this choir trip to Europe since joining the choir in seventh grade. Dad is so excited for me to go. But this is going to be a long two weeks.

I head home from the hospital and up to my room. My bags are carefully packed. I love my new luggage Mom and Dad gave me for graduation. We are allowed to bring one suitcase and one carry-on for our two-week A Cappella tour. Good thing they bought me the biggest suitcase in the store. I've had a lot to pack.

Jessica and I are going to be roommates and it's going to be so perfect. We've had our ups and downs throughout high school, but she is really a true friend. I am so glad we met in junior high. Melanie and Dana are going to be roommates too and if Jessica and her boyfriend, Steve, are too lovey dovey in our room, I can always go hang with them.

Somewhere in Europe,
a Few Days Later

I sit down on the hard wooden pew near the back of the church. Dan slides in next to me and just sits with me for a bit.

"Karen?" he whispers.

I look up and then over at my friend.

"Dan, what's up?"

"Look, Karen, I hope it's okay, but I think we need to pray for your mom in every church we walk into on this trip. What do you think?"

"I think it's a great idea, but I don't even know what to pray."

Tears start streaming down my face. Honestly, I don't even know how I have any tears left in my body. It's been a rough few weeks.

Melanie, Dana, Jessica, Steve, and Joe walk up and sit around us. Dan tells them that we should pray for my mom in every church and asks them to pray too. Everyone agrees.

"But she's so, so sick. I don't know what to pray. I want to go home in two weeks and find out that the cancer is totally gone."

"Then we'll pray for that miracle."

We sit together and I feel strength coming from these friends of mine as we pray together silently.

God. Please, please heal my mom. I want her back. I want her home. I'm scared, God. Amen.

After a few moments, Mr. Franklin calls us all to the front of the church for rehearsal.

"Thank you, guys. I didn't want to come but I am glad that I did. Let's make this the trip of a lifetime."

We all hug each other and head to the front of the church.

Somewhere Else in Europe, a Few Days After That

"Hey Karen, you wanna call home?"

"No, that's okay! I'll wait for you guys over here."

I sit on a bench across from my friends at the pay phones. Dana walks over and sits next to me.

"How come you're not calling home?"

"My dad told me not to."

"Why?"

"I think he wants me to just have fun and forget about what's happening at home. But that's hard. Especially when everyone else is calling home and laughing and hearing their parents' voices. I've got to get away from here."

I stand up because suddenly the air has been sucked right out of the whole area in the park where I'm sitting. I start walking. Dana follows close behind. I want to be alone, but I shouldn't be alone. She knows.

The Day We Return

"Dad! I'm over here!"

I wave frantically at my dad to come help me with my 647-pound suitcase.

"Welcome back and wow, I forgot how big this suitcase is. How was the trip?"

"Oh Dad, it was awesome! Every country was so beautiful. Jessica was the best roommate. Dana and Melanie were so much fun. Oh my gosh, Dana, Max, Ted, and I danced in St. Mark's Square in Venice, and we told people we were professional American dancers and they believed us! It was the absolute best! Every concert was so good. I want to buy all the cassette tapes. They are going to send us the information to buy them, but we have to buy them because you will love them. Dan almost got sent home! He overslept and missed the bus one day. Knucklehead. It was so great. I missed you though! I missed Mom too."

"I'm glad it was such a good trip."

"My bag is so heavy because I got souvenirs for EVERYONE. I got Mom a potholder from Germany. It was so beautiful there. She'll love it."

"Good, that's nice."

We load my bags into the trunk.

"We're going to the hospital right now. Mom will like that potholder."

I walk around to my side and open the door to get in. There is a card on the front seat with my name on it.

"What's this?"

"Open it."

It is a card from Sue and Pete congratulating me on becoming an aunt.

"What?! Sue's pregnant! That's so awesome!!! I'm going to be an aunt!"

"Karen, there's something else."

Dad is sitting in the driver's seat and turns to face me.

"It's about Mom. The cancer. The cancer has spread to her brain. So, we're going to go there right now because she's not doing so good."

"What? Oh, I knew I shouldn't have gone. She's worse."

I look out the window and blink back my tears.

"She's worse. I'm hoping she will know who you are. She doesn't always know who people are."

We ride to the hospital in silence. I am angry. Angry at myself for going. Angry at my dad for not letting me call home. Angry at Sue for telling me she's pregnant, knowing the next news is bad news. Angry at my friends for making me laugh and have fun on the trip. Angry at my mom for being sick. Angry at God.

That's right God, I'm pissed at you! Didn't you hear my prayers? Didn't you hear all of our prayers? Why didn't you answer them??? I shouldn't have gone, while I was laughing and making memories, the cancer attacked her brain.

I'm so mad, I can't even cry.

We pull into the familiar parking garage and start winding our way up and up to a level that has parking.

"I hate this place. I hate coming here."

"Me too, Karen, me too."

We park and I don't want to get out of the car. I don't want to go back into the hospital and back to her depressing room. I don't want to go in. I don't want her to be too far gone to know who I am.

I'm scared.

"Karen, come on now. Let's go see your mom."

Deep breath.

"Okay but let me get her potholder from Germany out of my bag."

I grab the potholder. What a stupid souvenir. What was I thinking? As if she's going to cook again. As if she's going to make me sloppy joe's or beef stroganoff on my birthday again. As if she's going to have all the neighbors over for a potluck again. Why did I buy such a stupid, stupid gift for her?

We walk through so many halls to her room. We are silent. Dad lets me walk in the room first, holding the stupid potholder. She is asleep. I stand at the foot of her bed and look at all the machines that are connected to her body. Her body that is wrecked. There's no way around it, her hair is mostly gone, there's a big cavern in her chest with melted skin covering where the first cancer had been. The chemo, the radiation that melted her, none of it worked. She is worse. I shouldn't have gone.

I stand at the foot of her bed holding my breath, holding my tears, and holding the God damn potholder.

She opens her eyes and barely says, "Karen."

I can't hold my tears any longer as I step forward and place the potholder from Germany in her hands.

"Mom, I'm here. I love you so much."

"Mommy."

"Yes Mom, I'm here."

Early July 1988

Mom is still in the hospital. Dad thinks she will be coming home but I don't know. I really hope she does.

Things are going really well with Matt. I like him so much. We talk on the phone pretty much every day. I wish he didn't live 40 minutes away so I could see him more often. His parents are pretty strict and I don't think they love that he's hanging out with an "older" woman.

Whatever. Tonight, we are driving with a couple of his friends down to The Taste of Chicago. His buddy's cousin lives kind of close to Grant Park so we can park in his alley and walk. I am beyond excited to do something fun and The Taste is always a good time. Food, people, food, the lake…hot guy I think I'm kind of dating. What could be better?

The guys pick me up and Matt and I are snuggled in the back seat for the quick ride into the city. We park the car, and the two guys are walking in front of us. Paul turns around.

"You guys are going out, right?"

I look at Matt. Oh boy. He hasn't officially said we are boyfriend and girlfriend, and this is all very new to me so I have no idea what to say or what to do. I blink. He looks at me and smiles the biggest smile.

"Yeah. Yeah, we're going out."

Then he pulls me into a hug and we hold hands as we continue to float, I mean walk, to the festival.

I've got a boyfriend. A real, genuine, bona fide boyfriend! This is shaping up to be the best summer of my life.

Well, except for the fact that cancer is running rampant in my mom's body. It is now in her eyes, bones, and brain—complete and total metastatic breast cancer.

Meeting My Mom

One summer day in July, that sweet, new boyfriend of mine comes with me to visit my mom in the hospital. Due to the cancer now invading her brain, we never know what a visit will be like. She hasn't been making a lot of sense in conversations and I give him fair warning.

Bless my mom though, and honestly bless Matt, because soon after we arrive, I explain to her that this was Matt, my boyfriend. She looks him right in the eye.

"Are you getting married?"

Oh boy! Thank God for his sense of humor and his kindness. He laughs nervously while I explain.

"Mom, no. We are just dating. Matt is going to be a senior in high school, and I am going to start college in a few weeks. He wanted to come and meet you today. Isn't that nice?"

"It is."

Then she nodded off and after a little while Matt and I headed out.

"Thank you for that. I know it's weird dating someone whose mom is so sick. It was really nice of you to come. I'm sorry for what she said."

"It's okay babe. I'm glad I got to meet her."

Holding On

Near the middle of the month, it is determined Mom is no longer able to stay in the hospital. Her cancer is too advanced and there is nothing more they can do for her. Now my parents have to decide if she comes home or goes to a nursing home. I'm kind of scared for her to come home. She's so, so sick. Dad told us that before the cancer went to her brain, she said she doesn't want to go home to die. She doesn't want that to be the last memory we have of her.

There is a room at a local hospital's nursing home that is attached to the hospital. The good news is that it will now be about ten minutes from our house. The bad news is that my 47-year-old, once vivacious, life of the party, mom is being moved to a nursing home to live out the rest of her life.

Seriously God?

I am in an absolute fog of terror. How did this come about? Can we tell my grandparents that their daughter has cancer yet? Dad seems to spend every waking moment at the hospital with my mom. I feel truly on my own and continue to fill my days with work at the video store, friends, and time with Matt.

I go to the nursing home the day she is moved. Dad and Sue are already here. The hallways are dim, and the colors all blend together in different shades of neutral blah. The smell of pee is strong and it's hard not to stare into every doorway that's open. Old man there, old lady across over there, old people everywhere. My mom is not an old lady for Christ's sake. She should not be here!

Why couldn't the hospital help her? How did they run out of treatments for her? A hospital that can't make someone better. What a joke. Best hospital in Chicago? I don't think so.

I know it's Mom's room before I get there. I know because I hear her screaming for help. I run. Why is she yelling? What is happening?

It's just been a few weeks since I got back from my trip, and she hasn't really made any noise since then. When she does talk, it doesn't make much sense. They said that's normal with brain tumors and we shouldn't expect her to make sense or really be with us ever again.

Good job, hospital.

I get to her doorway. Mom is writhing in her bed, screaming in pain. And no one is helping her. A nurse walks up and says there's nothing they can do; they are waiting on "orders." She shows us some hard, worn-out chairs we can sit in at the foot of her bed. We sit. We sit without talking and stare at her as she suffers.

I can't anymore. I stand up, no one looks at me. I am fuming. What do they mean they can't do anything else for her? They are doctors and she is sick! She'd hate it here so much. This is a nursing home for old people. She is not old. She's in so much pain.

I march to the nurse's station.

"Excuse me! My mom is lying in there and she is in pain, and no one is doing anything! Why isn't anyone doing anything? Where is her pain medication? She has cancer in her spine, her bones, her eyes, her BRAIN, and she is feeling it all! Why is she feeling it all? This is cruel! Where is her pain medication?!"

I'm gasping for breath, terrified, and angry. Angry that Dad is sitting mute. Angry that Sue isn't doing anything. Angry that Mom is in this horrible place when the hospital should be helping her— healing her. My anger spews right out of me onto this nurse who is just staring at me.

"Please. Answer me. Why is she feeling all of this? Why aren't you helping her?"

The nurse tries to hide her own anger.

"I know hon, I know. The hospital sent her to us, but they didn't send the prescriptions for her pain meds. We can't do anything until they get us that information. I know, hon, I'm sorry."

"Well how long will that be? She has cancer everywhere and she's so weak. Since it went to her brain, she's been gone from us. She's in so much pain and my dad and my sister aren't moving or talking in there. I'm 18! Why am I the one asking all the questions?!"

"I know, hon, I know. I'll be in with the meds as soon as I can. You hang in there."

She tries to give me a smile, but I don't want a smile. I want my mom to stop writhing and screaming in her bed. I want my mom to be better. I want my mom to know who I am. I want my mom. I want my mom. I smash my palms into my eye sockets to force the tears back in. Right now, I've got to be strong. I've got to solve this. I've got to help them get her meds for her.

"What can I do to help? How can I help you help my mom?"

"Oh hon, there's nothing you can do to help. You go help your dad. I'm working on this."

I don't want to go back into that room, but I know that I must. Mom has always, always needed me to be strong. She even used to call me "mom" sometimes. Oh, I wish I could hear her yelling from her bedroom, "Mommy, mommy, come quick!" I'd go running in and she'd tell me she needed a hug and a kiss or invite me to cuddle and watch an old movie. She'd ask me in a baby voice, and I'd oblige if I could. Or I'd tuck her in and tell her I was busy if I had homework, or a game I was in the middle of myself. Those days are definitely gone. I walk across the hall and back into her room.

We've got three stupid chairs at the foot of her bed. Dad and Sue are planted in two of them and they don't even look up when I come back in the room. Mom is crying and moaning.

"I went and talked to her nurse. The hospital didn't send any of her pain meds, or orders for them. I can't believe it, can you? She's in so much pain."

My dad nods. Sue tells me to leave the nurses alone because they're busy. I will not leave anyone alone. Mom is suffering. Can't they see? So much pain. So much agony.

Just as I prepare to stand to demand action from the doctors, nurses, anyone, Mom goes quiet. She turns her head and opens her eyes, staring at the empty chair on the side of her bed.

I hold my breath.

She speaks.

"Jesus, I'm ready. Take me with you."

I lean forward and stare at the empty chair. I squint because I want to see Jesus in the chair too.

"Jesus, I'm ready."

This is it. She's going to die right this very minute. She sees Jesus. But I don't! Jesus, where are you?

She keeps talking, calmly, coherently. To Jesus. She hasn't said anything coherent in the weeks since I got back. And here she is, TALKING TO JESUS HIMSELF! He is with her.

Mom keeps talking, and it appears that's she's also listening. I'm blown away as I watch this, and I know that I am absolutely witnessing something special.

Jesus, I know you're here. Heal her. Please. Heal her.

The nurse comes running in with her pain meds. Within moments her eyes close and she's asleep. The nurse gives me a nod. My dad and sister are still silent.

I will remember this moment as the exact time I literally felt the presence of God. My mom went from extreme pain and agony to a peaceful quiet. As I watched her face, it was smooth, relaxed even. She was looking directly at God, in the form of Jesus, who was apparently sitting right next to her in the empty chair. I believe he was leaning towards her, maybe even stroking her head, or holding her hand. She paused and listened.

What was God telling her? Was God there to bring her to Heaven? It was such a blissfully peaceful moment that felt entirely like it was captured in a precious and precarious bubble. The moments that she lay relaxed, and at peace, in the light of God, are moments I will never forget. My own heart rate slowed down, and I felt like I was looking in absolute slow motion through a lens of peace I'd never before experienced. I wanted her to let go and leave with God. But that wasn't the plan that day. God's plan never fails to amaze me. As much as I'd like to impose my plans on everyone around me, God reminds me that it's not up to me to make any plans at all. I can leave that to God.

August 1, 1988

Going to the nursing home daily is wearing on me and is so depressing. My mom doesn't know who I am and she mostly sleeps. Her hair is mostly gone, just patchy tufts. She is gaunt, even emaciated. So, I stop going every day.

Matt leaves town for his family's weeklong summer vacation. It's going to be a long week without him. I re-arrange my bedroom furniture again. I've moved my bed to the far end of my room, under the windows by the front of the house. I like it here because I can see my whole room and a little bit of light comes in from the streetlights outside at night when I'm lying in bed.

August 3, 1988

It's the middle of the night and I'm sound asleep when the phone rings. I wake up on the first ring and on the third ring, I hear Dad pick it up downstairs. This can't be good.

In just a couple of minutes, Dad is out the front door. I hear him get in the car and start it up. I sit up and part my blinds to look out as he drives quickly away. I want to go across the hall to Dave's room but remember he's not home. I take a deep breath and let it out slowly. I slide back under my covers and fold my hands over my chest. I want to pray. What should I pray for? I can't think of anything, so I just lay still and breathe in, then out.

God? Are you there? I am scared. I think something bad has happened to my mom. Are you with her? Can you be? I'm still mad at you.

I have no idea how much time passes but I'm lying up here, wide awake, staring at my rainbow mobile spinning around. I hear Dad's car. I don't move. I hear Dad coming up the stairs. I don't breathe. He comes in my room. It's dark so I don't know if he can tell my eyes are open. I stare at him as he sits down near the bottom of my bed.

"Mom died."

Then he falls forward onto my bed, sobbing. I am crying as I sit up and pat his back. He is just crying and crying, and I don't know what to do. I feel like I am the parent, and I am comforting him.

I barely whisper, "It's okay Dad. It will be okay."

But I don't believe it. I feel like I am going to throw up. Mom died?

"It's okay Dad. It will be okay."

He leaves my room after what feels like a very long time. I think he's going to make phone calls or something. I burrow down into my bed and hold my afghan close to me. I feel under my pillow and even bring out the last piece of my blankie I have left. I hold it all so tightly and cry until I don't think there is a drop of anything left in me to cry out.

I must have fallen asleep because I wake up and I feel like I've been hit by a truck. How does anyone even know what that feels like? I don't care. It's how I feel. My head hurts, my body hurts from being curled up super tightly all night long, and my heart hurts. My heart hurts so much. I uncurl my fingers from my treasures and stretch out my whole body.

Mom died. I should get up and go downstairs. I don't want to go downstairs. I should pray. I don't want to pray.

God, not now. I don't have anything to say to you.

I get dressed. I brush my teeth. I go downstairs.

I get to the bottom step and turn to see people sitting around the kitchen table. Everyone is crying. My aunt looks right at me and I start crying too. So much crying. Someone says they are making arrangements. I go back up to my room and check to see if the phone is open. I call Jenny and ask her if she can let our friends know that my mom died. Oh my God. My mom died. Mom is gone.

More family members arrive. I just feel numb. I don't want to eat, I just want to throw up. But someone gives me lunch and I eat it. I go sit on a couch in the TV room. Someone calls me from the kitchen.

"Karen, you've got a friend here."

What? Who is here?

"Joe?"

Joe comes into the TV room and gives me the best hug.

"I'm so sorry, Karen. Jenny told me and I just wanted to come say how sorry I am. I'm going to our farm later today and I won't be here for the funeral. I just wanted to come by."

"Thank you. Thank you for coming over. This means a lot."

"How are you?"

"I don't know. It doesn't feel real."

"I bet."

We chat for a few more minutes and my aunts in the kitchen are all pretending not to eavesdrop but they aren't good at it. Poor Joe.

"Let me walk you out to your car. I could use some fresh air."

We walk through the house. All the faces around me are a blur. Outside feels good. Joe leaves and I go back into the house. It feels so heavy in here. The air is thicker somehow. I'm heading back up to my room when I get called to the kitchen.

"Was that your boyfriend? Oh, he's so good looking!"

"No, that's my good friend. My boyfriend is on vacation with his family."

"Too bad! He's a cutie."

"My boyfriend is also a cutie."

I head to my room. I have no way to let Matt know that my mom died. All I can do is write him a letter to tell him what is happening. He won't be back until next week and the visitation and funeral are in a couple of days. I can't believe he won't be here for any of it. It's going to be a hard letter for him to get, but I don't know what else to do. I sit down at my desk, pull out some stationary, and start to write.

August 4, 1988

I ask Sue to come up to my room and help me look through my closet to see if I have anything I can wear for the visitation tomorrow and then the funeral. I don't. Sue, Pete, Dave, and I all go shopping.

For the visitation, I get a medium-blue dress with a mock turtleneck, shoulder pads, short-sleeves, wide patent leather belt around the waist. The dress hits below my knees and is pretty comfortable. I'll wear it with light pantyhose and my black, patent leather flats.

For the funeral, I get a black pencil skirt and a royal blue silk blouse with little black triangles on it. It's long-sleeved and has shoulder pads because, duh, shoulder pads make everything better. I'll wear nude hose and my black patent leather pumps.

My outfits are set. My heart is not.

August 5, 1988

Her visitation will be an entire day-long event. She had a lot of friends and was very involved in the community so the largest room at the funeral home is secured. I put on my new blue dress, jewelry, minimal make-up, and somehow arrive at the funeral home with my family.

Before things begin, we are ushered into a small room that feels very crowded. I want it to just be my siblings, Dad, and I. But, my mom's brother, his family, and my mom's parents are with us too. I don't like that. I want it to just be us. The casket would be closed, but we are asked if we want to see my mom before.

"No."

I look around at everyone else in the too small room. I am the only one who dissented.

Someone, I think on the staff of the funeral home tells my dad that it would be good for me to see, to know that it's all real. He turns to me.

"Karen, it's important that we all see Mom one last time."

"Dad, no, I don't want to."

Sweat is trickling down my back, but I am freezing cold at the same time. I feel a definite pressure to participate in this viewing of my dead mom's body. I don't want to go through that door and see her dead. I do not want to because maybe she didn't really die. Maybe she's in the witness protection program and all of this was done to protect her. Maybe I will see her again soon.

I do NOT want to enter that room. A part of me knows that I have to. The witness protection story probably isn't true.

Since she died, I have felt totally and completely out of my body. I hadn't been to visit her in the nursing home, didn't have a cherished "last memory," and my guilt is growing—literally multiplying by the moment. Plus there is no air left in this little room and I know, I just know, that I need to move through this and keep moving forward.

Someone opens the door to the next room, and I cannot look up. I am looking at my patent leather clad feet and I cannot look up. I will not look up. If I look up and see her dead then it's real. There are some gasps and people around me are crying. I feel how heavy the room is. I feel it and I don't want to look. But I know I have to look. I raise my head and see my mom.

She looks horrible, emaciated, so very sick. What little hair she had left is in patchy tufts. We chose the navy dress she wore for my brother's graduation. She loved that dress and now her ravaged body is lost in the fabric.

I didn't want to see her because I didn't want it to be real.

But it is. Too real. At 47 years old, my vivacious, bawdy, Muppet-loving, life-of-the-party mom is gone. No life left.

After a brief time, we leave the room. The casket is closed. Time to greet the masses.

My mom's friend, Mara, a local florist she often worked with, created a blanket of flowers to be draped over her casket in the shape of a pig. I don't know why, but my mom loved pigs and had been collecting them for years. Miss Piggy was her ultimate favorite.

This blanket of flowers, beautifully and creatively shaped as a pig, would have made her so happy.

The day is long and the line of mourners never seems to end. A couple of my friends, Jenny and Amanda, stay the entire day. When Jenny's family comes, her mom holds me tight and cries with me. Their family has given me so much stability and love in the last couple of years. I'm not sure they will ever truly know how powerful that is.

Matt isn't here but all of his friends come and tell me he would want them there. High school boys, stepping up and stepping in. I sure hope Matt will read my letter right when he gets home so he can know what has happened. Oh how I wish he was here.

More and more of my friends come. I am touched and feel every single hug and act of kindness.

Dan walks in. I break family ranks and walk straight back to the entrance to the room, stifling my sobs as I walk. I am so sad, broken really, that the prayers we prayed in five European countries hadn't worked.

Our old neighbor looks at me with sadness and says, "Today was rough honey, but tomorrow is going to be so much worse."

At the end of the night, my siblings walk up to me as I sit on a couch with Jenny and Amanda. They are holding the sign-in book and accusingly ask me if I knew how many of my friends came throughout the day.

"A lot."

"Over 85! How is that possible if we weren't supposed to tell people?"

"What? Do you mean you really never told anyone?"

I couldn't hide my shock and confusion.

Then, the night takes a turn I don't expect. Thank God my friends stay with me. Extended family leave the funeral home. Then my dad and sister say they are going out together for dinner with a group of friends. My brother is going out with his friends.

What? Our family isn't staying together for the rest of the night? Aren't we supposed to stay together?

For all of the plans that had been determined in the past two days, how has no one thought of what will happen when the visitation ended? Or had they? How were people considering leaving each other? What am I supposed to do?

I am the last to leave the building with Jenny and Amanda. We go to New Star Inn for Chinese food and then decide to stop by a house party being hosted by Rick Bandori.

Oh my gosh. Poor Rick Bandori. We aren't friends but he is part of the greater group of guys I spent time with the previous summer with The Pact. We ring the bell and when Rick opens the door, his face cannot hide the fact that he knows my mom has died and her visitation was that same day.

He lets us in with a smile, and as we walk through the house I leave my body. Heads turning, staring, so many friends that came to the visitation are here at the party. I think it is weird they are all still in their dress-up-visitation clothes but have lost all concept of time so who knows when I saw them at the funeral home.

I keep moving through the house and make it outside to the back porch. I now know it was a huge mistake to come. I can't seem to find any air to breathe. I feel sorry for bringing sadness to Rick's party. I want my two friends to be able to have some fun after spending a long, hard day with me. I stand on the porch in a literal daze. Some of my Orchesis dance friends bounce up, totally unaware of my loss.

"Oh my gosh, Karen, you look so pretty!"

"Why are you all dressed up?"

"I...um...I came from a visitation."

I look around, literally gasping for air.

"Oh my God, who died???"

"Um...my mom."

I know I have to get the hell out of here before I completely fall apart. I race inside, find my friends, and they drive me home.

They drop me off in the driveway and I let myself in the front door with my key.

I am the first one home. The house is totally empty.

The smell of lilies assaults my nose, stifling my ability to breathe yet again. How did all of the funeral flowers get here but no one is home?

It is all too much. I race through the house, up the stairs, and to the shelter of my bedroom sanctuary.

August 6, 1988

Today is the funeral. Everything feels thick, heavy, and so sad. I don't want this day to be real.

I go to church in an absolute fog of dread. They expect a full house for the funeral and because of the nature of the service, we sit in the first pew.

I am unsettled with this. Mom would have wanted us in the second pew, where as a toddler, I ate her entire tube of red lipstick like a popsicle. That second pew is where I would always try to snuggle up to her because she had such a pretty singing voice, and always smelled so good. I feel like an intruder sitting in the first pew. It is off. Mom sat in the second pew.

Our family files in, me first. Then my brother, brother-in-law, sister, and my dad. I don't want to sit on the end and move so I can be surrounded, touched on both sides. My sister immediately scowls at me. I am sure I'm messing things up in her mind. But I can't be on the end. I just can't so she will have to deal with it.

The closed casket rests in front of us. There are words and then the pastor looks at my dad, urging him up to speak. The emotions are too intense. Dad looks at him and then looks down. I wish I was sitting next to Dad to hold on to him, but there is no way my sister will allow me to scootch again.

I hold my breath as the pastor starts to talk about my mom and her life. Just moments after he begins, my dad stands, clears his throat, walks to the front, holds on to the lectern with both hands, and bravely eulogizes his bride.

I am just crying and crying. And when my dad speaks specifically about how proud my mom was of me—he names every accomplishment that I wasn't even sure she paid attention to in the years that she was sick——my sadness takes on a whole new level.

I realize in that moment that she saw me. Through everything she endured, she did see me. I think I am literally going to fall to pieces.

Amazing Grace is sung by a soloist which lulls my senses and puts me into a hypnotic state of sorts.

As the service ends, the casket is rolled back up the aisle, and we are supposed to stand up and follow it out. I didn't know this. How can I stand? How can I walk? As I stand and turn, I see all the sad faces looking at us, at me. I can't bear it. My dad puts his arm around my shoulder and guides me forward. I am crying so hard that I can't see. I swerve into a pew on the left and my dad rights me.

I blink back my tears, straighten up, and proceed forward with some deep gulps of air. At the end of the church, the casket is put in a hearse and drives away for cremation.

Watching my mom being forever driven away provokes such a feeling of despair, as if an actual piece of my soul is going with her. I am exhausted but now we have to go to the fellowship hall for a light reception.

I just want to walk home and go to sleep. But I guess it is good to see how many people knew and cared for my mom, my dad, and our family. That neighbor finds me, looks me right in the eye and says he told me the funeral would be worse. He is right.

Dad tells one of my cousins to take the pig flowers because she also collects pigs. I am worrying about her and how hard it will ultimately be when those flowers die. She is crying and nodding and can't easily speak as she gathers it up in her arms.

August 6, 1988, is absolutely one of the hardest days of my entire life.

I now have about two weeks to prepare for my freshman year at Bradley University.

A Positive Distraction

Just a few days after the funeral, I get a phone call. It is Matt.

"Babe! We're back from vacation and it was great. I can't wait to see you!"

He is full of energy and excitement.

"Oh. Um, did you get your mail by any chance?"

"My dad just left to go to the post office to pick it up. Why? What's up?"

I slide down the wall, clutching the phone close to my ear. I really wish he had gotten my letter before calling.

"I wrote you a letter. Um…while you were gone…my mom died."

To his complete and total credit, Matt gently wraps up our call and is at my front door as quickly as his parent's car would move him there.

Extended family is still in the house and I really wish I can have some serious privacy. Opening the front door, I just kind of fall into his arms and cry. I truly don't think I have any tears left. He is a trooper.

We walk to our living room and sit and talk about all of it. I tell him how his friends were all amazing and were all there at the visitation, and some at the funeral, representing him and being supportive and kind to me. He is a great listener, and I am glad to have him back home.

With time fleeting before we all leave for college, I am spending time having last moments with friends. One night, a group of my good friends plan a dinner out at a restaurant. We are all going to get dressed up and spend one last night together. I don't know what to wear so I grab the blue dress from my mom's visitation. It is comfy, and stylish (yay shoulder pads!).

Dinner out feels grown up and fun and is a much-needed relief from the torrent of emotions I have been enduring. After dinner, the conversation turns to what we can do next. Someone suggests I call Matt and see if we can hang out with him and his friends.

Wow, it hits me that I really do have a boyfriend and my friends want to hang out with him and his friends. We connect and meet up in someone's backyard where there are more laughs.

It is a great night of distraction, friendship, and genuine fun. I am grateful for it all.

Preparing for College

Even though I still feel like I am moving through some sort of a grief fog, it is time to prepare for my freshman year of college at Bradley University. My dad is an alumnus and I know he is excited for me to attend. Thankfully, Jenny is also heading there, and so are a few other high school friends.

It suddenly seems like I have a lot to do in a very short period of time. I am completely clueless. One of my godmothers, my Aunt Carole, picks me up one day and takes me to a wonderful store I have never heard of—Bed, Bath, & Beyond. Apparently, they will have everything a girl needs to head off to college.

Together we shop, choose bedding, towels, and a little caddy to carry my toiletries to the dorm bathroom. We fill a cart and enjoy lunch out at a restaurant as well. It is really a wonderful day with one of my favorite people. Mom and Aunt Carole grew up together and she was one of Mom's very best friends in the whole world. She sat right behind me at the funeral and put her hand on my shoulder more than once. She has always, always been a special part of my life and ever since I was a little girl, I have known how special she is and how lucky I am to be her goddaughter.

A few days after we go shopping, Dad and I go to visit my paternal grandfather at the nursing home where he lives. Grandpa is 88 years old and was not able to be at the funeral or visitation for Mom.

I am anxious about going to a nursing home after spending so much time in one with my mom being sick and then dying there.

But it is the right thing to go and visit and say good-bye to him before leaving soon for college.

We walk into his room, and I know he is glad to have us there. My dad uses an extra loud voice so he can hear him and tells his dad that I came to visit before leaving for college in a few days. Oh, Grandpa is having none of that.

"What? College? No! She can't go to college. She's got to stay home and take care of you."

"No Dad, she will go to college. That's the plan."

My heart sinks. Should I be going? Who will take care of my dad?

"It's okay Grandpa, Dad will be fine. I need to go to college."

Grandpa doesn't agree. Dad insists. I sit with a crushed spirit and tentacles of panic starting to grip my soul. Our visit is short and the drive back home feels extra long because now I'm really worrying if I should go or not.

"Dad, are you really going to be okay if I go?"

"If you go? Oh, you are going. There is no question."

"But will you be okay?"

"You're going."

And that was the end of the conversation.

Back at home, I begin packing my things. I am heading off to actual college, majoring in Radio & TV. I have high hopes of becoming a game show host and this seems the best path forward. In all honesty, I haven't given choosing a major much thought at all. I am constantly "on" and entertaining the people I am with. Radio/ TV seems to be the right fit. I am planning on auditioning for the choir, rushing a sorority, and immersing myself in the world of college. Staying busy, moving forward. My grief is raw but forward motion seems to be the logical thing to do. So, I move forward.

Matt and I agree that we will stay a couple but decide not to be totally exclusive. Well, I am ready to be exclusive. Are you kidding me? I finally have a boyfriend and he is pretty great. But we are crazy realistic and aren't in love, yet, so we say we'll stay together and see where things go. I'm pretty sure they are going to go great, and we will stay a strong couple.

In a matter of days, I will be off to Bradley, settled into my dorm room in University Hall, and begin the process of sorority rush.

Karen Goes to College

It's mid-August, time to head out, and Dad's Oldsmobile is packed and ready to deliver me to my freshman year. Our destination: University Hall, floor 4a, one of the coveted Dorms of the Future!

Yes, I drew the dorm lottery prize and that means my room is equipped with a personal computer (PC if you're in the know) for my roommate and I to share. This is groundbreaking and really my first foray into using computers. We certainly don't have one at home—who even does? Students are told to bring our own floppy disks and our lives will be infinitely simpler and...futuristic.

My roommate, Kimberly, and I are both from the suburbs of Chicago and hit it off when we meet. She tolerates all my Big Top Pee Wee cut-outs and brightly colored decor. I couldn't take my rainbow room with me to college, but I can certainly bring the vibe.

Sorority Rush is the first week on campus. Bradley has six national sororities, and I don't know much about any of them. My dad's fraternity brothers from Bradley mostly married women from one specific house, and I do have that in mind.

I am assigned a rush counselor and spend the week attending various events at each house. At the end of every round, I will narrow down my choices, and the houses will narrow down theirs.

One house continually stands out to me because each time I walk in and meet someone new, they are unique from the last person I met. While other houses seem to have some sort of mold to fit, in my eyes Pi Beta Phi does not. They quickly rise to the top and I am hopeful I'll continue to be invited back.

Besides rush happening this first week, my social life is taking quick form. Jenny lives just below me and her roommate, Cindy, and I bonded along with some other new friends on both of our floors.

By bonded, I mean we gather together almost every night talking and drinking.

I am lucky that I am never cut from a house. I feel that the power to choose is in my hands and I know others aren't so lucky. Each day, we get the news as to which houses invited us back. Every day, there are tears scattered throughout the dorm and campus in general. It is intense.

I am grateful for the distraction that it is. I find being alone almost intolerable. So, I constantly seek out other people to keep my mind anywhere but on the fact that Mom is gone.

The night before the final round, the Preference Round, my friends and I overdo it. One of my new friends and across-the-hall neighbor convinced her parents to let her come to school with a blender. For "smoothies." Our smoothies are strawberry daiquiris and boy do they taste good. They taste so good, I drink more than I should.

I wake up the morning of Preference Round and I feel horrible. I got invited back to two houses. Pref is a fancy dress-up day and if you are lucky, you get to go to two houses—one for lunch and one for dessert. I am excited to head first to the sorority of my dad's friends' wives and second to Pi Phi.

U-Hall has communal bathrooms. On this particular morning, I gather up my yellow, personalized shower tote, robe up, and gingerly make my way down the hall to shower.

I don't feel well at all.

Midway through my shower, I feel lightheaded. The next thing I know, I am on the shower floor, the upper part of my body thrust outside of the curtain, rudely interrupting the primping of the other girls on my floor. There are a few screams. Only one girl comes over to help me. She has obviously been crying.

"Hi. Are you okay? You don't look so good."

"Hi. Thanks. I don't feel so good."

"Let me help you."

I sit up and pull my towel around me.

"It's okay. I'll be okay. You can go get ready. It's a big day."

"Oh, I don't need to get ready. I was double cut. No Pref rounds for me today."

"I am really sorry. That sucks."

"It really does. You don't look good at all. I think you need to go to the Health Center."

The next events are fuzzy. I get to the Health Center and it is assumed I fainted because of menstrual cramps. So, I am given a prescribed muscle relaxant.

Have you seen the end of the movie Sixteen Candles? Where the bride takes muscle relaxants for cramps?

That is literally me.

Because of all of this, I miss the first sorority lunch. Thankfully, Pi Phi is second on the docket and my first choice. I get dressed, yet again in the blue visitation dress, do my hair, put on my make-up... in a completely drugged state. I don't think I have ever been more relaxed. My arms feel heavy but do everything I tell them to. I'm more than ready.

My mom taught me that early is better than late, and even better than on time. It is raining. I grab my umbrella and set off across campus. Once at the house, I simply stand under my umbrella on the sidewalk.

I notice no one is around. I'm feeling really good, really, really good, so I don't mind. I stand and wait. Apparently, there is a break between groups, and I am really early. But no worries in my mind, I want to make a good impression. I am oblivious to the swishing of the vertical window blinds as curious eyes keep peering out at me.

I have absolutely no idea that by standing solo, early to the party, I give the impression that I am a rogue rushee who boldly chose only one house to attend on this final day. This creates a big buzz.

Eventually more girls show up, I am feeling extremely groovy thanks to the muscle relaxant, and the party begins. Towards the end of the party, I feel like I'm coming back into my body again. I don't feel quite so groovy and am concerned that I've made the wrong impression. I really like Pi Phi and I'm sure the other house is mad I didn't show. I find Jenny's roommate, Cindy, and we walk back to our dorm together.

"I missed the first party. I basically passed out in the shower when I was getting ready. I had to go to the Health Center and got the same kinds of pills the bride had in Sixteen Candles!"

"Shut up!! How do you feel now?"

"Better. Embarrassed, but better."

"I hope Jenny is doing okay."

"What do you mean? Is she sick too?"

"Didn't you hear?

"Hear what?"

"She got double cut."

"No way! Jenny is awesome! She is sweet and kind and beautiful. Are you kidding me?"

"I wish. She was so upset when I left."

"Oh my gosh. Jenny was one of the most popular girls in our high school. This doesn't make any sense at all."

Cindy and I go with our other dorm pals to meet with our rush counselors to rank the houses we visited first and second. Then I go back to my room, change out of my dress, and go right down to Jenny and Cindy's room. Jenny is a mess. I can tell she's been crying all morning. I don't know what to say so I just hang out with them in their room. We are all shocked.

Later in the day, Cindy and I meet up and head to the field house for Calling Out. This means we are both in a house, but we don't know which one. We are nervous and excited, and both hope we get Pi Phi.

"I am so nervous and so excited. I am also so glad I feel normal again!"

"Same!"

I find my rush counselor and am bummed to see she's not a Pi Phi. I like her! She's in the house where every girl looked exactly the same and all wore pearl necklaces. Oh shoot, I'm pretty sure I made that comment to her this last week when I cut them from my list!

"Karen, are you feeling better?"

"So much better, thank you! And hey, I am sorry about what I said about your house this week. Everyone was nice, it's just that…"

"Listen, you were exactly right about what you said. No hard feelings! Here's your bid. I think you're going to be happy!"

She hands me my envelope and I open it up. I AM A PI PHI! I can't believe it! I didn't scare them away with my weird actions today. I make my way through the sea of freaked out, excited girls and find my new dorm pals. Eve, Andrea (blender friend!), and Cindy (Jenny's roommate) are all in Pi Phi too. We hug. We scream. We jump up and down.

The rush counselors corral us all together by house and each group goes into the field house. All the Pi Phi rush counselors are with us now and this is really happening! It's so loud in here because hundreds of girls are cheering and screaming. We all run across the stage and jump down into the arms of all of our new sisters. This is intense and wonderful. The only thing that would make things better is if Jenny were here too.

The Dream

I am sitting on an old, brown, metal folding chair. I look down and see that it is the kind my grandparents would bring out when company came. The sun is shining brightly, and my body feels warm as I look forward and see the greenest grass. Beyond is a small pond and the water is still.

It is peaceful.

I look next to me, and Mom is sitting right there, in another folding chair. I realize that we are in a park—but wait, it's a cemetery that feels like a park. Mom is quiet and looking around, just like I am. It feels so good to be with her.

It is peaceful. I feel calm.

She turns her head and looks right at me. She smiles and it is so, so good to see her smile again.

"It's okay. You're going to be okay. Everything will be okay." Mom shares this with me so matter-of-factly and I believe her.

It is peaceful. I feel calm. I miss my mom.

At that precise moment, I open my eyes. It is the middle of the night, the only light in my dorm room is from my brand-new-grad-gift fancy digital alarm clock. I don't have my glasses on, and things are blurry. Looking down at the edge of bed, I sense my mom.

She is sitting at the edge of my bed. I wonder if Kimberly can see her too.

"Kimberly," I whisper loudly, "Kimberly!!!"

"What, what?"

Kimberly is in a sleepy stupor.

"Is my mom sitting at the edge of my bed?"

BIG MISTAKE

Big, big mistake.

Sweet Kimberly lets out a blood-curdling scream, jumping to her feet on top of her bed, and starts screaming.

"Sweet Jesus, sweet, sweet Jesus!"

She rapidly claps her hands to coincide with the run-jumping action of her body. I scared poor Kimberly to her bones. Now I am also frightened.

I tell her about my dream and that I felt certain my mom was actually there with me. This doesn't help her calm down at all. Not one bit. Once we settle back in to hopefully fall asleep again, I pray for the first time in a really long time.

Okay God, that was pretty intense and really scary. I don't know what that was, but maybe my mom shouldn't come back like that again.

A few days later poor Kimberly lets me know her friend would like to move in with her next semester. Maybe I could find another room? My good pal Lynn-across-the-hall needs a new roommate, so it will all work out.

Matt's Demise, October 1988

College is fun! Matt and I are still a couple and before I left we agreed to date around a little if we wanted. I totally think this is meant just for me. He goes to an all-boys Catholic high school. Who is he going to date? Plus, we're pretty solid. We've been through a lot, and honestly, I can't believe that hasn't scared him away. I've made out with a couple of guys, but Matt is still definitely my boyfriend.

One day when Matt and I are talking on the phone, the topic of his Homecoming dance comes up.

"Babe, about the dance. I think I'm going to ask Katie Hancock."

"Um, she sleeps with all her dates."

"Yeah, I know."

I am crushed. Katie Hancock? Ouch. She is someone I consider a friend. We were on Drill Team and the Orchesis dance team together.

"Okay, you can go. But promise me you won't have sex with her."

"Okay babe."

I continue on with college life. I go to most of my classes, but not really German. Why did I take German? I've never taken German before and it is so hard. Easiest if I just avoid it all together. Jenny, Staci, Lynn, and I all become Little Sisters at the same frat and we party and dance every weekend, all weekend, and sometimes during the week too.

The Homecoming dance comes and goes. Matt and I are still officially a couple. Life is pretty great.

MEDIUM

LOW · HIGH

MOXIE METER

Rumors start to swirl back home that Katie and Matt did indeed do the deed the night of the dance. Jenny's younger sister is friends with Katie and is hosting a big sleepover. On the invite list is, you got it—Katie. Jenny and I do the logical thing. We drive home from college for the weekend. Another good friend does the same. We meet in Jenny's bedroom the afternoon of the sleepover and hatch our plan.

We put a blank cassette into a tape recorder and my two besties slide right under the bed with the loaded listening device as the party gets underway. I seek out Katie and bring her up to the room for a chat.

My friends hit the record button just before we enter the interrogation room. I can sense her nerves but continue. I repeatedly ask her if she had sex with Matt at his Homecoming and it doesn't take long for her to confess, bursting into tears.

I truly am not upset with her at all. I actually like her. But she did sleep with my boyfriend and that is unfortunate. After her tears dry and we are wrapping things up, we both hear a loud click.

"What was that?"

I knew that the recording had run out of tape and automatically clicked off. I pretend to not hear anything while she looks around the room nervously.

"What was what? I didn't hear anything. Look Katie, you can head back to the sleepover. I think it was really dumb to have sex with Matt. I thought we were friends. But whatever."

Then I usher her right out the bedroom door. My friends roll out from under the bed with the evidence freshly recorded.

After that dramatic weekend, I go back to college where I continue to drink blender drinks, dance in the frat house basement, and mostly go to class. I drive home again soon and don't tell Matt I am coming.

It is time for a confrontation.

I find Matt at a house party, well actually, a detached-garage party. I stroll in, heart racing, and see him with a beer in one hand, a cigarette hanging from his mouth. I completely surprise him, and he almost swallows that cigarette.

"Babe! Babe, wow, you're here."

He comes in for a big kiss and I dodge.

"Yeah, I am here. Can we go for a ride?"

"Sure! I didn't know you were coming."

"I know."

I guide him to my dad's Delta '88 Oldsmobile, all decked out with power windows, power locks, and…a cassette player.

We drive around for just a few minutes.

"It's good to see you."

He tries to hold my hand.

"Thanks."

"How's school?"

"Fine."

I pull the car over and park. I take full advantage of my dad's car and its many fancy features. I hit the power lock button which genuinely startles Matt. I unbuckle my seatbelt and slowly turn to my passenger, adding great dramatic effect in my mind. Then I simply ask him about Homecoming.

"How was the dance? Truly?"

"Good."

"I see. Did you have sex with Katie?"

"Babe. No, babe I would never do that to you."

"Are you sure?"

"Babe."

"Really, really sure?"

He nods an emphatic "No."

At this point, I lean over and open the glove compartment. I pull out the cassette, take it out of its holder, push it into the player, and hit play. He listens and then tears start to stream down his face. It is so dramatic and so fantastic.

I totally forgive him. We aren't in love, we agreed to see other people. Does it feel good to have him go that far? Absolutely not. Was I willing to go that far with him? Absolutely not. Well, at least not until Christmas break but whatever.

I drive him home and stay chatting with him and his brother for several hours. We break up before I leave. My first official boyfriend is history.

I didn't ever tell Matt the main reason that I drove home this weekend. It's time to bury Mom's ashes. I think it is weird that it took this long, but what do I know? Dad picked out a spot in a cemetery that's kind of far away. He likes it because it's more like a park. All the headstones are down flat on the ground. When you drive around, it isn't supposed to feel like a cemetery. But it still feels like a cemetery to me. There is a big windmill and Dad loves that. In front of the windmill there is a little pond and in front of the little pond is a spot where all of the cremains are buried. There is a marker with both Mom and Dad's names and birth years. Mom's death year is marked and Dad's is open. I think that is creepy. But again, what do I know? I can't wait to get back to school and my friends and the fun.

I drive back to college and am going to stay at school until Thanksgiving break. I find that whenever I sit down to actually study, my mind gets calm, I remember that my mom is gone, and the tears come. I decide I need to stop those tears from coming because once they come, it is so very hard to stop them. I absolutely won't allow myself to break down and find all kinds of ways to distract myself.

If I'm studying when the tears start, I close my books and head out to find the fun. It isn't hard. If friends in one room are studying, I'll skip to the next. I keep going until I can find somewhere to land.

Being a Frat Little Sister

Probably my favorite part of college so far is being a frat little sister. I am assigned a Big Brother to navigate the process and look out for me. Naturally, mine is one of the better dancers and is an absolute pro at the tight roll of his jeans. He has a slightly southern-Illinois accent that has him pronouncing my nickname "Mod" as "Maude" and it is endearing. He really is a nice guy and I feel lucky.

One day, I am sitting upstairs in the frat living room area and a real looker strolls in. A wave of heat rolls right through my body, and a voice, clear as can be shouts in my head: YOU'RE GOING TO MARRY THAT GUY.

I am intrigued. The problem is, this hot guy is dating someone, and I am kind of friends with her. Bummer! Good thing campus is full of other cuties to grab my attention and keep me fully distracted from the mundane things like going to class and studying. I will say: this hot guy is on my radar.

One task Little Sisters are expected to accomplish is to get the signature of every guy in the house on the wooden paddle that our Big Brothers gifted us with. At this time in my budding college career, I am skipping down the stairs in my dorm and miss the bottom step. I am laying on my back at the bottom of the stairs and people are just stepping around me. I know my ankle is messed up and I sit up carefully.

"Hey! Anyone! Can anyone help me get down the rest of the stairs?"

Most people walk by but a couple of girls stop and help me. Thankfully, the security team on campus is able to drive me to the

ER and I return with torn ligaments on my right ankle and a shiny pair of crutches. I am devastated that I can't participate in aerobics any longer and also not too sad that I am able to legitimately miss classes for a few days.

This injury does not deter my quest for signatures at the frat house, and especially my newfound mission of getting to know hot guy who, by the way, is also a junior. I've never even considered such an older guy, but college is different and there is something about this guy.

I tuck the wooden paddle under my chin and crutch around that frat house like a champ. I specifically crutch carefully to room 13 and flash a dazzling smile at hot guy and get that coveted signature, my heart racing the whole time. He's even hotter up close!

It takes a while to meet all of the guys and during that time I decide I need to get more face time with the junior. I respect the fact that he is in a relationship. I admit that I find the match a little odd and don't think it will hurt to seek him out again, flip my paddle to the other side, and get his sexy signature just one more time…

End of Semester One

My first semester is flying by. I never miss a party at the frat house. I understand that I have classes, but I often choose to skip them. I learn that I could fake symptoms so well that the university health center will even skip testing me and simply diagnose me with Mono. That note gets me out of class, "legitimately," for at least a week.

The holidays begin to loom, and Dad decides our family of now four, plus my brother-in-law, will head to the magical city of Orlando for the week before Christmas. It will be a good distraction from missing Mom and by now, I am becoming an expert at distractions.

One of Dad's friends offers up their condo for us to stay in and we board a plane and head to fun in the sun. My sister is seven months pregnant and has really been through a lot of stress with her pregnancy. Her doctor told her she absolutely could go but must rest and use a wheelchair when possible.

We spend our days pushing her around SeaWorld, Disney World, and Epcot. One day, we are at The Magic Kingdom and Pete is pushing her down Main Street. One of the wheels gets stuck in a trolley track.

"Pete! Pete, I'm stuck!"

A trolley can be spotted in the far distance, and she starts to panic, encouraging her husband to get her unstuck and off the tracks. My brother and I start laughing and shout at her to simply stand up so that he could lift the chair and move it to safety.

There is just something so silly about that moment that really has us laughing and laughing. It feels like a great release to be together, distracted, having a solid laugh.

While on this trip, we also get to visit my dad's aunt and uncle. She is my grandma's sister and they don't have any children of their own so they are definitely bonus grandparents to us. We don't get to see them often but when we do, it is always very special.

This trip shows me how important time with family is and I am grateful for yet another distraction to keep me from the sadness that continues to grow within me. I really, really miss my mom. I can literally feel it weighing on my heart.

Our family arrives home just a few days before Christmas. We always spend Christmas Eve with Mom's side of the family so we head to my aunt and uncle's house. Christmas Day is always spent with Dad's side of the family so on the 25th, we head to my other aunt and uncle's house. All nine of my cousins, plus spouses and dates, are there. I smile my way through it all. My sadness is there, and it isn't talked about. We are all putting on a happy face and giving it our best. I don't know what "it" actually is, but I do genuinely appreciate my extended family.

As my semester break winds down, I start searching out the mail each day before Dad can get to it. My grades will be coming soon, and I know there is no possible way I could have done well. Panic starts to set in. Luckily, I get to them before my dad. It is bad. The worst grades I have ever gotten, a 1.87 out of a 4.0. I do what any terrified teen would do: I hide them from my dad. Before break is over, Dad remembers to ask about my grades.

"Dad, they're not good. It was a hard semester."

"What do you mean not good? Show me."

"No, Dad, you don't want to see them. Trust me. They were bad but I'll do better. I promise."

"SHOW ME!"

I dig out my first college report card and hand it to him. I can't look at him. He is furious. I start crying.

"I promise I'll do better. I promise!"

"You'd better."

I drive back to school and have no idea how I'm going to do better.

January 21, 1989

I wake up feeling kind of glum. I am an eighteen-year-old girl who lost her mom to cancer, broke up with my only real boyfriend (because he had sex with one of my friends), the weather is dreary, and I am down. My high school friend, Jess, is visiting for the weekend and she's hungover and sound asleep.

I write her a note, grab my car keys, and do what any other college freshman in 1989 would have done—I go to the mall, walk in to a hair salon, and get a perm.

It is a glorious perm and just looking at myself in the salon mirror, I am already feeling better. I bounce out of that salon feeling like a new woman ready for action. I drive back to my dorm and get lots of oohs and aahs from everyone I encounter on my way back to my room.

The plan for the night is to go to another frat party at the same house we always party at. Why go anywhere else? Free beer, excellent dance music, and the hot junior I have a crush on is now single. This freshly permed girl is up for a night of dancing!

My friend across the hall has the cutest clothes. She lends me my outfit for the night.

It is everything I dream of in an outfit. I don a pair of kelly green stir-up leggings, which (of course) comes with a matching kelly green mock turtleneck top with shoulder pads. I then add the final piece of the coordinating outfit, a matching black sweater with large, primary colored, polka dots…and more shoulder pads. I finish the look with chunky black socks and black, lace-up granny boots.

I. Am. Ready.

The night before, Jess and I were at the frat house, laughing about the fun we had this past summer when we toured Europe in choir and specifically discussed piercing our friend Steve's ear.

Jess and I hit the scene. We are dolled up and ready to be dancing in the house basement to Erasure, Depeche Mode, Billy Idol, all of our favorites.

I am freshly permed, fully shoulder padded, and ready to take on the world.

Out of the corner of my eye, I see my biggest crush, now single, walking towards me. I can not believe it.

The perm must have worked!

"Hey. Do you know anyone that can pierce my ear?"

"Um, yeah. I can. I can pierce your ear!"

"Okay great. Meet me in room 13 at 2:00."

"I'll be there."

2 a.m. rolls around and I am ready for some ear piercing. I head to room 13 with Jess close at hand. There is a line of guys in the hallway. They tell us they are all in line because they heard some girl is going to be piercing ears and they want in. What?! Well, it doesn't matter to me.

Hot junior is waiting, and he talked to me, and I have a new perm and I am wearing my favorite color, and I am having a great day!

A large safety pin is secured. A quick pass over the open flame of someone's lighter guarantees it is sterile, and I tell him to take a seat on his desk chair so I can pierce his ear.

I try. I try. I try some more. But I really have a crush on this guy and I don't want to hurt him. At one point I am actually squatting on his lap trying so hard to get that pin through his lobe.

I cannot do it.

After what seems like an eternity, but is likely five minutes, another pal takes the safety pin, jams it through his earlobe, and fastens it on the other side.

Thank God for Jess because she somehow clears the room, hits the lights, and then dissipates the line out in the hallway.

It is at that precise moment that Mike Brothers and I share our first kiss.

And let me tell you, it is some kiss.

Meeting the Parents

After several months of dating and officially being in love, it is time to meet Mike's parents. We load into his Bronco after class on a Friday and roll into rural Beecher, Illinois around 9:00 p.m.

I have never really driven in the country, and it is the beginning of a whole new set of experiences that I will ultimately file away as "Trips to Beecher." For starters, it is quiet and so very dark. His town has a sole stop light, and I don't think we see a single other car as we cruise right through the town part of Beecher. Mike explains that his good friends live in town, and we will meet them the following day. He says we have four miles to go out to his house in the country. The country! How exotic!

The road is flat and smooth, and did I mention dark? No streetlights anywhere and Mike laughs out loud when I ask about them.

"Why would there be lights on the streets? Everyone knows where they are going."

"Well, I don't know where I'm going and it's friggin' dark out here. Are we in the actual middle of nowhere?"

Mike laughs and my stomach flips, which I am certain has nothing to do with nerves and is all about how much I love this guy with his wavy brown hair parted down the middle, and his Girbaud sweaters. What a catch and I am so happy that he is MY catch. I am going to meet his parents in a few short moments! After four miles, we turn on to a very bumpy road.

"What's up with this road? Why is it so bumpy?"

"What? Oh, all the country roads don't get paved."

"Why?"

I am perplexed.

"Why would they need to be?"

He responds, equally perplexed.

We soon pull into a very long driveway and come to a stop in front of a two-story, dark house. Why is everything so dark?

Mike turns to me and says, "Don't be nervous. You'll be great!"

"Why is it so dark?"

"My parents are probably already asleep."

This is my first red flag. I ignore it as we walk right into the unlocked front door.

I whisper, "Why isn't the door locked?"

Mike whispers back, "Babe, we're in the country. No need to lock the doors."

And I'm thinking to myself, Of course not, the roads aren't paved. Who the heck would drive out here??

The house is totally dark except for a pale light in the front hallway. His parents are indeed asleep. That's right, asleep at 9:00 p.m.! I was already nervous to meet them and am honestly shocked that they are asleep. My parents would have been in the prime of their evening TV watching. My mom might have even been sitting around a neighbor's table over cigarettes and coffee at 9:00 at night. My parents certainly would have waited up to meet my boyfriend for the first time. At NINE O'CLOCK! Mike grabs my hand and leads me towards the stairs.

"What room am I staying in?"

He laughs.

Mine, silly."

Wait, what?

"I can stay with you in your room?"

"Of course. Where else would you stay?"

Mike shakes his head as he laughs quietly.

"Um, a guest room? No way you'll be allowed to stay in my room when you meet my family."

Mike turns off the hallway light and grabs my hand, leading me up a tall stairway. His room is at the top of the stairs on the right. He flips on the light, and I suck in my breath. Could it be?

"You've got a waterbed?"

I am in a state of blissful shock. How lucky am I? I love waterbeds! They are warm and comfy and only the coolest of parents get their kids a waterbed. I forgive his parents for being asleep as I snuggle in with my love in his fancy, waveless, waterbed for a good night's…sleep before meeting his parents in the morning.

It's at this point of the story that I need to remind my reader that I was, and still am, a nighttime person. As a kid, I'd stay up until 2, 3, or even 4:00 in the morning watching TV, reading books, latch-hooking a rug, it didn't matter. I was always awake and at my best in the darkness of the night. As a result, I sleep in. This first Saturday morning at my boyfriend's house, with his parents awake before the crack of dawn and waiting to meet me, is no exception. Plus, the waterbed is super warm and comfy!

I wake up around 10 a.m., alone in Mike's room. I get dressed, use the bathroom in the hall, and decide to do a recon mission quickly and quietly into his parent's room. I use all of my childhood super sleuthing tricks and slide oh-so-quietly into their space. There is a dresser full of framed photos and I am able to quickly discern who his parents are before heading down the stairs. The photo is a bunch of adults, and everyone is smiling and laughing.

This family must be like mine, I think before heading down the stairs.

Midway down the stairs, I hear a woman's rising voice.

"Don't be a smart fart!"

I stop in my tracks and hold my breath. What did she just say? Did she just call someone a "smart fart"? Did she just say the word "fart"? I am intrigued and terrified. In all my nineteen years on this earth, the word fart was presented as a four-letter F-word. We were absolutely not allowed to say it. EVER.

I don't know what to do. Should I retreat back to the warmth of the waveless waterbed, or continue down the stairs and meet this woman who said fart out loud? I have no choice. Mike hears me and meets me at the stairs. He introduces me to his mom and dad, Irene and Arnie.

"Hi, it's nice to meet you."

I put on a big smile as I take in the scene. His dad looks the same as the photo, but his mom does not. It was obviously from many years prior and her long hair in the pic is now super short and cropped to her head.

"Hi there," Arnie says with a nod.

"Aren't you a late sleeper?" Irene says with a head tilt.

Then it happens. A single event that will throw the rest of the weekend off the rails.

I sneeze.

Irene and Arnie jump into action.

"Are you sick?"

"Here's a tissue!"

"Get the NyQuil!"

I am taken aback.

"Oh no, I'm not sick. I've got allergies. No big deal."

It is too late to put the train back on the tracks. Arnie leaves the room and comes back with a huge bottle of NyQuil.

"Here you go young lady, take a big swig of this. It will knock the cold right out of you."

Arnie hands me the bottle. I put up my hand.

"Oh, no, but thank you though. It's just a little allergy thing. I'm fine."

It is past the point of no return with Arnie as he takes a plastic cup off the top of the bottle and pours a full shot of the syrupy medicine into the cup and hands it to me.

"Drink it young lady."

Again, I put my hand up as I look for Mike to help. He is nowhere to be seen. His dad is trying to drug me, and he is gone. Is he alive? Did they drug him too? Is this even his dad? Yes, yes, it's his dad because he was in the picture upstairs. Oh my God, what is happening?

"No, no thank you. I've never had NyQuil before. Isn't it for nighttime? I just woke up. I have allergies. But thank you."

I try to decline but Arnie puts it right into my hand. I feel I have no other choice but to slam it down as Mike walks in.

"Dad, she's fine, it's just allergies."

"Well son, the NyQuil will knock those allergies right out of her."

Arnie means well. Within the first five minutes of meeting my boyfriend's parents I take my first ever shot of NyQuil. We then eat a big breakfast, and I answer questions politely as I try to wrap my head around the fact that his mom says words like fart and his dad basically poured drugs down my throat. And the roads aren't paved. What fresh hell is this place?

After breakfast, Mike takes my hand and tells his parents we are heading to town to meet the Hansons. John Hanson is a few years younger, and Mike tells me he is like his brother and his parents are really a second set of parents for him. I am happy for a change of scenery but am starting to get a little sleepy. No worries though, I can push through and meet this important-to-my-boyfriend family.

Don and Helen Hanson are an absolute delight. They live in town, on a paved road, and are very, very kind. We sit at the kitchen table visiting for a bit and then Don wants to show Mike how he's made their basement into a man cave. Giant, console TV with a huge, dark, velvety sectional couch. It feels like a movie theater. I get cozy, snuggle up next to Mike and am suddenly overwhelmed with yawns. I apologize as I fight to keep my eyes open.

The next thing I know, I start to wake up from what feels like the heaviest sleep of my life. I have no idea where I am. It is incredibly dark, and I try to focus my eyes. I am soooo groggy. I blink myself fully awake and realize as I sit up that the entire right side of my face and the hair on that side of my head is soaked in my drool. Where am I? Then it comes to me. I am still in the Hanson's basement on their brand new, now drool-soaked couch. Oh my gosh. I look over and see a crack of light under the closed basement door at the top of the stairs.

I wipe off my face and wring out my hair (not really). I get up and walk up the stairs, mortified that I fell asleep at the house of this really important family to Mike. And I didn't just fall asleep. I was unconscious and I didn't even know what day it was anymore. I turn the knob and slowly open the door, peeking my head out.

"Hello sleepy head!"

Helen greets me in her cheerful voice. I look around the kitchen table and see Mike, Don, and John all seated with an apparent card game going on.

"Um, hi. I am so, so sorry. I don't know what happened. I think it's because Mike's dad drugged me."

I respond with a small smile. Mike walks over to me as Helen is shocked.

"He drugged you? What on earth? Mike?!"

I quickly answer, "No, no. Not real drugs. But I sneezed once because of my allergies and he made me drink NyQuil and it was morning and…"

I hold back tears.

Mike says, "Why'd you drink it? You didn't have to take it."

"I wanted to be polite. I just met him, and you weren't around so I didn't know what to do." I am still exhausted. "What time is it now?"

Don laughs, "It's after 8:00!"

"At night?"

I am mortified! We arrived before noon!!

"At night!" everyone says in unison.

"I'm afraid I drooled all over your new couch. Can I please have a towel to go wipe it up?"

Helen comes and puts an arm around me.

"Well, you sure know how to make a first impression don't you?"

She laughs and together we go down and mop up my catatonic drool puddle.

For a while there that day, my moxie was unconscious. But then, it woke right back up again and forged new friendships.

Lavaliered, Pinned, Engaged, Married

Mike Brothers and I are inseparable. Once I confess my horrific first semester grades, he becomes extremely serious about me getting back on track by assuring me he needs me to stay at school so we can be together. I need no further motivation—this guy has a waterbed! So I switch majors from Radio/TV to Elementary Education. I was a great babysitter and always loved kids. Plus, my elementary school experience was truly excellent. I wanted to take parts of all of my teachers (except Miss Jones from kindergarten) and become a positive influence in the lives of kids.

Greek life at our university is really strong and we are both quite active in our fraternity and sorority. There is a tradition when you are seriously dating someone that the guy would give the girl his fraternity letters in the form of a necklace. This is called a lavaliere. It means you are going out. If things keep getting more serious, he would give you his fraternity letters in the form of a pin. This is called getting pinned and it means you are basically pre-engaged, very serious. And then the next step is an engagement ring, which thankfully does not involve his fraternity letters at all.

In my sorority, if you achieved any of these relationship milestones, you kept it a secret until the next chapter meeting or social event. Then on the morning of the meeting/date party/ formal, you would place a poem about what the relationship means to you anonymously in the mailbox of the sorority president. At the meeting/event, the president would announce there would be a candlelight ceremony. All of the members would stand in a circle, cross arms, and hold hands. The president would read the poem. Then she would light and pass a votive candle while everyone sang the sweetheart song. The candle would pass around the circle once for friendship. The second time, if you left the poem and you were lavaliered, you would blow the candle out when it got to you. The third go round if you were pinned, and the fourth if you were engaged. Let me tell you, the excitement level truly built with each time the candle started the circle anew.

Mike and I are lavaliered at the end of my freshman year and pinned my sophomore year. His fraternity has the tradition of walking over to the lucky woman's sorority house and serenading her with their sweetheart song and a dozen red roses after the chapter meeting is over. It is always a big deal, and so exciting.

December 7, 1990, is a huge night. It is the night of my sorority formal and Mike has already graduated from undergrad and is in a one-year Master's degree program a whole state away from me. My roommate works nights at the local Fairfield Inn, and our whole crew of friends gets a block of rooms.

The night is spent dancing and partying with our friends. We get back to our hotel room and I kick off my uncomfortable heels and make a beeline for the bathroom.

"Mike, my contacts are killing me. I've got to get them out."

I go directly to the sink, fill up the little contact holder with solution, and place each contact lens in its home for the night. I then turn on the cold water and lean down to splash some on my face. As I flip my head back up and grab for a towel, Mike Brothers slides into the bathroom behind me and presents a small, dark box in front of me.

"Will you marry me?"

I am stunned. I can't see. Water is dripping down my face. I scrunch up my eyes and pull the box towards my face. It is a ring! It is a gorgeous, diamond ring. I turn around and throw my arms around my about-to-be fiancé.

"Yes! I will marry you!"

After some spectacular kissing to celebrate, I ask him why he popped the question in the bathroom.

"I got to the room earlier today. I couldn't find an ice bucket for the bottle of champagne I brought so I filled up the bathtub with ice and chilled it in there. We got back from formal and you went right to the bathroom. I panicked! I was afraid you'd see the champagne and know what was up."

"Oh babe, I couldn't see anything, not even this beautiful ring!"

And so, we are engaged. About a year and a half later, on June 6, 1992, we get married at the wonderful church at the end of my block where I was baptized, confirmed, and had my mom's funeral.

Standing at the back of the church, on my dad's arm, I take a deep breath as he slowly walks me down the same aisle just a few years earlier he was practically dragging me up behind my mom's casket. My moxie is infused into me with each step forward that we take, my eyes locked on the man I love so deeply.

The ceremony begins at 5:00 p.m. because I want soft candlelight to flank my arrival. All three of my godparents are up on the altar, ready to read different Bible verses we have chosen.

As my dad and I make my way down towards Mike, I make eye contact with the friends and family in attendance. I feel so strong and beautiful.

When we get to my groom, my dad does the hand-off, and right before we turn to walk up to the altar, Mike smiles at me, looks down a bit, and says something I will never forget.

"Where'd those come from?"

I glance at my padded chest.

"They come off with the dress."

I return the smile, we both exhale, and climb the few steps toward the rest of our lives together.

EPILOGUE

To clarify, Mike Brothers knew I did not get a boob job between the rehearsal dinner the night before and our wedding ceremony. He knew how hard I had worked to plan a perfect day; he knew I was a bit exhausted, and he believed I was nervous. He wanted to make me laugh. He did. We've been making each other laugh ever since.

ACKNOWLEDGEMENTS

As I've thought about who to thank for supporting me in this book, it seems like I should name every single person that was mentioned throughout the book. But we changed all their names and that would blow their identities! So, to all my childhood friends, my teachers, my high school friends, my college friends, my extended family, and my neighbors—I would not be who I am without the contributions you made to my life, thank you.

Families can be such a blessing and trust me, mine absolutely is. **Courtney**, **Kaylyn**, and **Olivia** this book is really for you. I hope you always hear my voice in the pages. I love you. **Mike Brothers**, we've been through so, so much. I wouldn't change a single thing. You are absolutely my favorite and I love you like crazy.

Dad, **Dave**, **Sue** and **Pete**, I love you and am thankful you are my people. **Mom**, I miss you. You are woven closely into my stories, tucked right where I need you to be. Your spirit absolutely lives in your seven granddaughters and it's fun to see you in each of them. You've got some great-grands now too and I see you in the literal sparkle in their eyes. You are so loved.

To my **Light Writers**, you truly supported me and believed in me when I didn't know how to believe in myself. What an absolute gift you have all been to me. I believe in each of you and the gifts you must share with our world.

My friends **Dawn**, **Staci**, **Paula**, **Heather**, **Lisa**, **Kori**, and my cousin **Julie** have all buoyed me when I felt adrift.

To the gals of my **Gaggle**, your constant encouragement has been deeply valued and treasured.

MOXIE MATTERS

How lucky am I to have enduring friendships throughout my life? These past decades have been made immeasurably richer thanks to **Shay**, **Sue**, and **Caryn**. You're deeply imprinted on so many chapters of my life.

Friends are a beautiful gift. Another gift in my life was finding a brilliant therapist! **Deborah K.**, thank you for listening thoughtfully and equipping me with the tools to shine a light on the layers of my messy, muddled, and magical life.

I am truly grateful to authors, coaches, and friends, **Bob Goff** and **Kimberly Stuart** for giving me valuable guidance and encouragement that is actually hard to describe. To my fellow **Writer's Workshop friends**: My name is still Karen, and I am cheering so loudly for each of you. Thank you for choosing to be in the same place, at the same time, so our lives could intersect in ways many of us never imagined possible.

The team at **Blue Hat Publishing** chose to partner with me and I sincerely could not have asked for better human beings to guide me through the process of publication. You have been a gift to me in more ways than you know. Thank you so very much.

Finally, this book is also dedicated to the memory of my childhood friend, **Katie Tomaso**. May heaven serve up unlimited OJ-7's and Wheat Thins to a truly beautiful friend and crime-solving playmate.

MAY YOUR DAYS BE
FILLED
WITH
MOXIE

MEDIUM

LOW

HIGH

MOXIE METER

(RATE **YOUR** MOXIE!)